His Proper Post

His Proper Post

A Biography of
Gen. Joshua Lawrence
Chamberlain

By Sis Deans

Belle Grove Publishing Company
Kearny, N.J.
1996

© 1996 Belle Grove Publishing Company
All rights reserved
Printed in the United States of America
Library of Congress Catolog Card Number 95-083643
ISBN 1-883926-07-6
For permission to reproduce selections from this book,
write to:
Belle Grove Publishing Co.
P.O. Box 483, Kearny, N.J. 07032

Dedication

I dedicate this book in the memory of Chief Petty Officer Edwin Lee Deans who served in the United States Navy during World War II, Korea, the Cuban Missile Crisis, and Vietnam. To his country, he was a dedicated serviceman; to his family, he was a gentle and loving man.

Fair winds and following seas, Pa

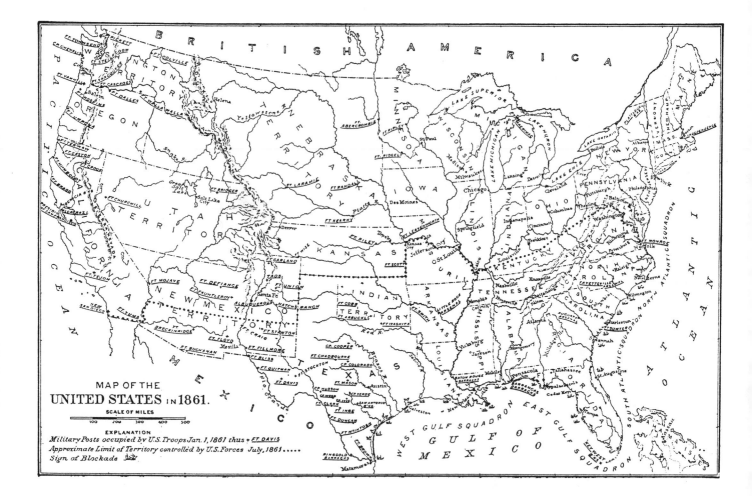

MAP OF THE
UNITED STATES IN 1861.

SCALE OF MILES

EXPLANATION

Military Posts occupied by U.S. Troops Jan. 1, 1861 thus + FT. DAVIS
Approximate Limit of Territory controlled by U.S. Forces July, 1861 ......
Sign of Blockade

Table Of Contents

Foreword

Every culture needs heroes. Stories of heroes remind the old and pass onto the young the characteristics and values which society cherishes. In Western culture, a traditional hero is an untried youth who goes on a journey in which his mettle is tested again and again. In his travels he encounters temptations and evil enemies which he destroys through his courage and virtue. His journey allows him to prove himself and at the same time make the world a better place. At the end of his journey, he returns to the place of his birth. Older, wiser, tested and strengthened, he becomes a counselor to whom the ordinary person may come for guidance.

Today, it is widely reported that Americans have no heroes. In other words, the values that cement us together are becoming more elusive. To find heroes, we are looking back to our history for American men and women whose characters and lives will reassure and help us define more clearly who we are.

Joshua Lawrence Chamberlain answers this need. Chamberlain was born in a small town in Maine, into an ordinary family. From his parents he learned the virtues of honor, discipline, patriotism, spiritual-mindedness and the ability to directly confront and master challenges -- like a severe stutter. He spent his youth preparing to do some good for the world, at that time thinking of becoming a missionary. The Civil War became his Odyssey where he was tested and proved he could not only do his duty but excel. By participating in the war he helped free the country from slavery and make it a better place. After the war he returned home, and became a governor, an educator, a statesman and a business man whose wisdom and counsel was frequently sought.

Speaking to the veterans of the 20th Maine a quarter-century after the War, Chamberlain spoke of developing that kind of character which allows ordinary people to become extraordinary, or heroic. "We know not of the future and cannot plan for it much" he said. "But we can hold our spirits and our bodies so pure and high, we may cherish such thoughts and such ideals, and dream such dreams of lofty purpose, that we can determine and know what manner of men we will be, whenever and wherever the hour strikes that calls to noble action."[1] He continued to discuss the value of character in defining heroism. "It is character that tells" he said. "I do not mean simply nor chiefly bravery. What I mean by character is a firm, seasoned substance of soul. I mean such qualities or acquirements as intelligence, thoughtfulness, conscientiousness, rightmindedness, patience, fortitude, long-suffering and unconquerable resolve."[2]

A man of character, Chamberlain is an American hero. His ideals and values are those which many Americans hold dear. Chamberlain believed in God and his Country. He believed in America's divine destiny to do good for the world and the power of the individual to make a difference for good. And he acted upon his beliefs. A man of integrity, a man of courage, he got the job done right without compromising his principles. Like us, Joshua Chamberlain was an ordinary American. He had weaknesses and failings. Yet, throughout his life he worked to be a more perfect person, to do God's will, and to live in service to others.

He succeeded remarkably well. In 1889, in speaking to the veterans of the Twentieth Maine, Chamberlain recognized that the difference he and the other veterans made fighting for their principles would be a lasting one. He said, "This is the great reward of service, to live, far out and on, in the life of others; this is the mystery of the Christ, -- to give life's best for such high sake that it shall be found again unto life eternal."[3]

This book will introduce you to a great American, Joshua Lawrence Chamberlain.

Julia Colvin Oehmig
Curator
Joshua Lawrence Chamberlain Museum
Pejepscot Historical Society
Brunswick, Maine

1. Chamberlain, Joshua L., Dedication of the Twentieth Maine Monuments at Gettysburg, October 3, 1889
2. Chamberlain, Joshua L., Dedication of the Twentieth Maine Monuments at Gettysburg, October 3, 1889
3. Chamberlain, Joshua L., Dedication of the Maine Monuments at Gettysburg, October 3, 1889.

Part One:

Do it; That's how!

Joshua L. Chamberlain's boyhood home near Brewer.

Childhood

"It was a matter of character...formed in the silent and peaceful years by the mother's knee and by the father's side, which stood you in such stead in the day of trial."

-Joshua L. Chamberlain to the Veterans of the 20th Maine Regiment, 1889

It was a muggy June day. All morning the sun had slipped in and out of a graying sky. By the time my three young daughters and I entered Pine Grove Cemetery in Brunswick, Maine, the sun had disappeared for good behind a wall of clouds. We had come to this small, quiet cemetery, edged with pine and dotted with tall oak and maple, to find the resting place of Joshua L. Chamberlain. Just as we discovered where this great man was buried, a wind picked up from the east, and a much needed summer shower began to fall.

I once read that as a young boy Chamberlain discovered that he could identify trees just by listening to the wind moving through their leaves. The swishing leaves of a nearby maple, whose branches reached like protective arms above his grave, reminded me of that story. It seemed right to me that he was buried in a place where pine, oak, and maple majestically stood, where, in the wind, their different songs could be heard.

One would think that Maine's greatest Civil War hero would have a large monument to mark his grave--a stone that would stand out among the others, one that would note his military honors, his four terms as governor of Maine, and his presidency of Bowdoin College. But the pinkish colored stone that marks his grave is small and simple. Only his name and the years of his birth and death are etched into the Maine granite. It was his wish to have nothing more.

Joshua Lawrence Chamberlain, whose given name was Lawrence Joshua, was born on September 8th, 1828. His father named him after James Lawrence, the captain of the American warship *Chesapeake*. During the War of 1812, after being wounded, the dying captain had urged his men to continue the fight with a line that quickly became famous: "Don't give up the ship!" Although Chamberlain would always be called Lawrence by his family and close childhood friends, while he was at Bowdoin College, he started going by the name of Joshua--his father and grandfather's name. Thereafter, he kept his first name as a middle initial.[1]

The year Joshua was born, John Quincy Adams was serving as sixth president of the United States, and for more than two million black people, life in America meant slavery. Back then, Bangor, Maine was famous for its shipbuilding and known throughout the world as a lumber port. Walking along its busy streets, one would have seen rugged lumberjacks muscled from felling 150-foot pine trees, tan-faced river-drivers who navigated logs down the rough waters of the Penobscot River, shipbuilders sporting leather tool belts, and sea captains and sailors from countries all over the world. Across the Penobscot River from Bangor was the small town of Brewer, also known for its lumber, shipbuilding, and woodburned bricks made of Brewer clay. There, on a one-hundred-acre farm, Joshua grew up.[2]

The oldest of five children, Joshua had three brothers--Horace, John, and Thomas--and a sister, Sarah, who everyone called Sae. His mother, Sarah, was a woman of great wit, and Joshua loved her dearly. With a gentle but firm hand, she made sure her children were well mannered. A woman of strong faith, she also made sure that religion played an important role in the Chamberlain home, and every Sunday, the whole family went to the First Congregational Church in Brewer where strict rules governed good behavior. For Joshua, going to church meant more than listening to the gospel, it meant music, and that was something he took great pleasure in.   Not only did he like to sing, he loved to listen to the local singing teacher play the bass viol. Having a quick and inventive mind, and wanting to learn how to play the instrument, he created one out of a cornstalk and some string, and used a willow branch for a bow. With this, he taught himself the basics and when he finally got a real viol, he practiced until he became an accomplished player.[3]

Joshua's father, a farmer and well-respected citizen, believed in hard work and clean living. Considered a good judge of timberland, he was occasionally hired to explore and survey uncut territory. Young Joshua often went along on these trips, traveling with his father, by canoe and on snowshoes, through the northern wilderness of Maine and Canada. This is how Joshua said he first learned to "camp out."[4]

Although Joshua's father taught his children to think for themselves, there was never any question as to who was boss. When he told them to do something, they did it, even if it seemed impossible. A perfect example was the time Joshua and his father were loading hay in one of their fields. Joshua's job that day was loading the hay and driving the wagon while his father raked up behind. They had about four hundred pounds of hay on the wagon when Joshua, who was not paying attention, got one of the front wheels stuck between two tree stumps in the bed of a stream.

"Clear that wheel!" his father shouted.
"How am I going to do it?" asked Joshua.
"Do it; that's how!" ordered his father.[5]

Sarah Dupee Brastow Chamberlain   **Joshua Chamberlain, Jr.**

Knowing his father was not going to help him, and angry with himself for not paying attention in the first place, Joshua grabbed the hub and yanked the wheel with all his angry might. He yanked it so hard that when the wheel cleared the stump the cart-tongue punched one of the oxen in the nose, and the team got out of the stream bed in a hurry. "Do it; that's how!" would be a saying and an attitude that would stay with Joshua Chamberlain his whole life.

Growing up on a farm in Maine meant half the year was spent preparing for winter and the other half getting through it. From the time the rooster crowed in the morning until it was too dark in the evening to hay, there was always work to do. Fences needed to be built and mended; gardens planted, weeded, and harvested; fields hayed; livestock tended; water hauled; trees cut; wood chopped and stacked for winter. Joshua, like his brothers, shouldered his share of the responsibilities and on occasion he had to improvise in order to get the work done. One illustration of this ability to improvise occurred when Joshua told his father that he and his brothers couldn't move a large rock that needed to be cleared from the field. "Move it!" was his father's only suggestion. How Joshua and his brothers figured out a way to "move it" is still a mystery, but when his father returned to the field the rock was gone.[6]

Despite his chores and schoolwork, Joshua managed to have some free time. Often he would visit families of the Penobscot tribe who camped in birch-bark wigwams near his father's land. They told the young boy stories of their ancestors and of the fierce fighting Mohawks. They shared with him their spiritual beliefs and legends that had been passed down through generations. He learned their language and seemed to be influenced by their way of life, for although young Joshua was a natural hunter and good with a rifle, he, like the Penobscot, never killed game for sport. He also developed a respect for nature and spent hours exploring the woods, studying trees, flowers, and wildlife. Because it would have been embarrassing for a boy his age to admit he was in the woods for that sole purpose, he said he almost always carried his rifle with him, hunting being an acceptable excuse.[7]

The Penobscot River, which stretches in length for 350 miles, also occupied much of Joshua's time. One attraction was the shipbuilding yards of McGilvery and Stetson where the ring of hammers could always be heard. The vessels built there eventually made the 24 mile trek out to open sea, but before they were launched from the Brewer banks, Joshua climbed up the main mast of every vessel and hung his hat on it. Growing up on the river, it was only natural for young children to learn to swim and sail at an early age, and Joshua and his brothers were no exception. Having heard the family stories about his grandfather Joshua (whose shipbuilding business had been destroyed when the British sailed up the Penobscot during the War of 1812), it is no wonder that he and his younger brothers liked to pretend that the *Lapwing*, their family's small boat, was really a warship. One can imagine Joshua and his younger brothers winning many victories against imaginary British vessels, avenging their grandfather and defending their country in the process. No doubt "Don't give up the ship!" was a favorite command.[8]

Another favorite pastime for Joshua was riding his mare. He said the two would go on "wild, unbridled racings over the rough back fields" taking "reckless cuts at full speed through the labyrinthine woods" and "flying leaps over the high brush fences."[9] His knowledge of horses and his ability to ride would prove valuable, and would, in the war years to come, save his life more than once. Another boyhood influence that would have an effect on those future years was his family's military background.

On his mother's side, both of Joshua's great-grandfathers fought in the American Revolution. One of them, Captain Thomas Brastow Jr., also fought in the French and Indian War. On his father's side, Joshua's great-grandfather, Ebenezer Chamberlain, was a soldier during both the French and Indian War and the Revolutionary War. His paternal grandfather, Joshua Chamberlain, was a colonel who at one time commanded the garrison at Eastport. Although a farmer, his father was also active in both civic and military affairs, serving as County Commissioner and as a lieutenant-colonel during Maine's Aroostook War with New Brunswick, Canada.

Coming from a family with such a strong patriotic and military background it is not surprising that Joshua's father sent him to Major Whiting's military academy in Ellsworth. There, at the age of fourteen, Joshua learned military drills and excelled at his schoolwork. Having a gift for learning languages, he easily picked up French and began studying Latin, just two of the many foreign languages he would eventually master. Unfortunately, while Joshua was at the academy, his father had some financial problems. Joshua returned home and, to help bring in money, took a job in a brickyard, and later, took another job making rope.[10]

Once the family was again financially stable, the question of Joshua's future became a debated issue between his parents. His mother wanted him to study the ministry at Bangor Theological Seminary; his father saw for him West Point and a military career. Joshua would go on to fulfill both wishes, but at that time, he was not interested in either one--he could not see the sense of an army career in a time of peace, and the life of a minister did not appeal to him. Wanting to please his mother, he said he would consider the ministry only if he could become a missionary in some far off place like Africa, "where he could take part in civilizing a people and help them to live right in this world."[11]

Because he was still young and had time to figure out what he really wanted to be, the only final decision Joshua made about his future was that he would go to Bowdoin College. Meanwhile, he attended the local school, where the teacher was also a doctor. Whenever the teacher, Dr. Pollard, got called away to treat a patient, he left either Joshua or another boy named Frank Arey in charge of his class. One day when Frank was filling in for Dr. Pollard, Joshua acted up in class by giving a "surly answer." Frank Arey called him up to the front of the room where he rapped Joshua's hands with a ferule (a stick used for punishment) until they were numb. Frank also told him,"...if you show any more of your insolence to me, I'll thrash you so your folks will not know you when you go home." A few weeks later, when Joshua was left in charge of the class, he caught Frank chewing tobacco, and although Frank was bigger and two years older, Joshua gave him a good "flogging" for it. Sixty-five years later, General

Joshua Chamberlain would run into Captain Frank Arey on Congress Street in Portland, and the first thing Joshua asked after saying hello was, "Do you remember the day I flogged you for chewing tobacco in school?" Captain Arey's reply was, "Yes, and I got what I deserved."[12]

Just after he turned eighteen, Joshua, wanting to save money for college, taught school in North Milford for a winter. Because it was too far from Brewer to commute, he boarded with a family whose home was described by one writer as "already crowded and quite rowdy."[13] Although he was not much older than some of his students, he managed to keep the troublemakers in line by winning their respect. He was not only a good teacher but one who wasn't afraid to dish out punishment if it was deserved, a fact Frank Arey could attest to. While in North Milford, Joshua also started an evening singing school which quickly became a popular way to court. Young people came from miles around to socialize and learn new hymns, accompanied by Joshua on his bass viol.

When the school term ended, Joshua returned home and began preparing for college. Gaining admission to Bowdoin was very difficult; he had to resume his study of Latin and learn Greek before he could even apply. But Joshua was determined, and once he set his mind on a job, he just did it. In a room he built in his parent's attic, he studied continuously for nine months. Each day he would write up a grueling work schedule; every hour from five in the morning until ten at night was filled. With the help of two tutors, one for Latin and one for Greek, he tackled his studies relentlessly. Through long hours of hard work, he memorized and was able to recite, word for word, Kuhner's unabridged Greek grammar.[14]

Finally, in February of 1848, Joshua, with his Latin tutor William Hyde, set out for Bowdoin in a one-horse sleigh. Tied to the back was a big wooden trunk and pulling the sleigh was Joshua's faithful mare. Recalling that trip, Joshua described himself as "a green and pale looking lad."[15] He had good reason to be afraid. Waiting for him at the college was a committee of professors who had agreed to examine him as a special favor. If he passed the test, he would get to unpack his trunk and become a Bowdoin student. If he failed, it would be long ride home.

Joshua Lawrence Chamberlain in 1857.

To Bowdoin And Back

"Bowdoin College has been preeminent, not as a writer of books; not even as a trainer of scholars, but as the mother and maker of men; men of personality and power and public leadership."

                                        -John Minot, <u>Tales of Bowdoin</u>, 1901

The day my daughters and I visited Chamberlain's grave, we also visited Bowdoin College. We were greeted with music. Through an open window of one of its ivy-clad buildings came the sound of a piano, from another window, a violin. Simultaneously, two different songs were being played, the piano flowing like a rapid river, the tender violin, a sleepy stream. The campus was as lovely as the music. Stately trees fence it off from the streets beyond and shelter it from noise. Groves of pine trees shade the pathways where Henry Wadsworth Longfellow and Nathaniel Hawthorne once walked as students. The architecture of its solid old buildings, built mostly of brick and stone, gives it a flavor of history and provides a rich atmosphere for learning.

Named after Massachusetts' Governor Bowdoin, the college first opened its doors to eight freshmen in September of 1802. In February of 1848, a future president would be admitted as a student: after a long journey and a nerve-wracking exam, Joshua said he learned "sometime in the dead of night" that he had been accepted.[16]

Months of studying and determination had paid off, but the joy of Joshua's accomplishment was tinged with some sadness. Entering Bowdoin meant leaving behind his family, the farm, and, in a sense, his childhood. His feelings about this are reflected in his *Early Memoirs* when he writes about his faithful mare who had brought him to Bowdoin. With sorrow, he realized that when she returned home without him the next day, neither of their lives would be the same. No longer would they share those wild rides of his youth, for on the road he was about to travel, "her fearless affection could not follow." About their parting he further wrote: "...the boy with things unspeakable in his heart, patted the silken whirlpool on her shining neck, whispered into those sensitive ears thoughts they could not hear, and gazed into those luminous, dark eyes mirroring depths which neither knew!"[17]

The following day, at six in the morning, Chamberlain began classes. During his college years at Bowdoin, he earned numerous awards for high grades and gained the respect of his peers and professors. These honors did not come without hard work. Math was a difficult subject for Joshua; sometimes he had to stay up all night to solve assigned problems. An even greater challenge for him was overcoming a speech impediment that had plagued him since childhood.

Joshua managed to keep his stuttering a secret from his professors and classmates at Bowdoin by avoiding words that began with p, b, and t, as words beginning with those letters he said, resulted in "horrible stammering." He was very sensitive about this disability. He said what most people took for "bashfulness" was really his reluctance to speak for fear of running into some dreaded word that would cause him to stutter. He was also terrified of having to read aloud in class and would scan ahead to prepare himself for any dangerous words in case he was called on. He was always on guard, always painfully aware of the risks of lengthy conversations or giving answers to questions during class. Especially embarrassing for him were those times when it was necessary to introduce friends whose first or last names began with the feared letters.[18]

Although Joshua became skillful at using synonyms, there were times when that tactic didn't work. By substituting words, sometimes what he was trying to say was not only misunderstood but sounded "stupid" even to him. It was a humiliating situation. He writes in his *Early Memoirs*: "Such a condition was intolerable. It was not a thing to be avoided, but to be overcome. . . . The thing now was to 'do it'."[19]

Joshua figured out two ways to conquer his speech impediment. One way he said, was to "get a good breath behind it [the word] and turn on the will." He explains the second method this way:

> If you are coming to something which you can't speak, persuade yourself you are going to sing. Catch the pulse of time. Feel the emotion of it, and that will bear you on its motion. If the occasion is a great one, let your whole spirit be possessed with the trance, and give itself freely to the rhythmic sway and swing. . . .It is not necessary to do this so badly and unskillfully as to draw the attention of your hearers from the things you are saying to the way you are saying them. That would very likely bring a laugh upon you and break you down. But you need not be ashamed. Anything that is worth saying, is worth singing. Let fools laugh if the wise learn. The Spartans used to sing their laws for after dinner pastime. And the Spartan laws were no laughing matter.[20]

Thus, instead of avoiding his speech impediment, he began attacking it with two weapons of his own invention. In his Memoirs he further states, "Some space has been given to this subject because it was a serious one, an experience which affected habits and perhaps character, and the indirect effects of which may have reached into the whole of life. The writer of this knows that obstacles irremovable can be surmounted."[21] He indeed surmounted this disability, eventually becoming an elegant speaker whose voice was described as "strong and resonant and used with perfect art."[22]

Another obstacle that Joshua would overcome during this time was an illness that left him delirious with fever while he was home on school break. The lingering illness was so severe that the family doctor did not believe Joshua would live. But Sarah Chamberlain was not about to give up hope. She fired the doctor, hired a homeopathic physician, and, with diligent nursing and loving care by her and Sae, Joshua slowly got better. It took nine months for him to fully recover, and he had to stay back a year at Bowdoin. Of his illness, Joshua said, "the patient learned patience."[23]

By summer, Joshua was himself again and said "for once a real vacation was enjoyed at home, among the fields and woods, and birds and beasts, held so dear."[24] By fall, he was back at Bowdoin.

Until he entered college, Joshua had never read a novel. His strict parents had forbidden that kind of reading while he was growing up. Although they put no restrictions on the Bible, text books, or even poetry, his parents considered novels to be mind-corrupting and immoral. As an assignment for one of his classes, he read and wrote a report on Nathaniel Hawthorne's House of the Seven Gables. This introduction to literature undoubtedly had an effect on him, for while at Bowdoin, Joshua would become involved with two literary groups. One was the Peucinian Society, for which he used to write poems; the second was The Round Table.[25]

Members of The Round Table met every two weeks to read and discuss their work. He said these works "were prepared with great care," for the members of the group were excellent writers and took their work seriously.[26] It was through The Round Table that be became a friend and admirer of author Harriet Beecher Stowe, whose husband was one of Joshua's professors. Of the two he writes, "a new great orb had risen on the eastern horizon in the person of Professor Calvin E. Stowe, with his Hebrew literature, and his genius of a wife--surely a double-star, this!"[27]

While Joshua was a student, Harriet Beecher Stowe, an abolitionist, was in the process of writing Uncle Tom's Cabin, which first appeared as a serial in a Washington D.C. antislavery paper, *The National Era*. On Saturday nights, Joshua and other members of The Round Table would go to Harriet's house where she would read and they would discuss her latest chapters before she sent them off for publication. About these chapters Chamberlain writes: "the author was least of all impressed with their merit, and surely no one there dreamed of the fame that was to follow."[28]

Like Stowe, Joshua had grown up in an era where slavery was legal in the South. By the time he entered his second year at Bowdoin, fifteen out of thirty states were slave states. Having been born and raised in Maine, Joshua had never seen slaves being sold on an auction block, but in the South it was an everyday occurrence. Treated like cattle, slaves were often forced to exhibit their bodies, teeth, and physical strengths for potential buyers, and it was not uncommon for wives to be sold away from husbands, or children from mothers if the sale meant a good profit. Living in the North, Joshua had never witnessed the atrocities of slavery, but his awareness of this unjust and inhumane way of life was certainly heightened by knowing the author of Uncle Tom's Cabin. Of Harriet, he writes: "The sweetness of spirit, and her genuine interest for others...were what drew to her the hearts of all."[29]

Joshua's disapproval of slavery was rooted in his religious beliefs, and while at Bowdoin, he continued to be active in the church. He taught Sunday School, attended religious meetings, and worshipped at the First Parish Church where he conducted the choir. The young boy who had used cornstalks to learn the viol also taught himself to play the organ as a college student and in his senior year became the organist for the college chapel.[30]

It was at the First Parish Church that Joshua first set eyes on the minister's beautiful daughter, Frances Caroline Adams, whom everyone called Fannie. Dark haired and spirited, Fannie had been adopted as a young child by Reverend Adams and his wife Sarah Ann. Her real parents, who lived in Boston, were Ashur and Amelia Adams. Ashur, who was old enough to be Fannie's grandfather, felt that a younger couple could provide a better family life for his daughter. Thus, when Fannie was about four years old, he made arrangements for her to live with his married nephew in Brunswick, Maine. Leaving her real home at such a young age and being separated from her older brothers and sisters must have been both confusing and hurtful for Fannie. Although there is no evidence that she was ever legally adopted, Fannie soon came to consider Reverend Adams and Sarah Ann as parents. Having no children of their own, Reverend Adams and his wife considered Fannie a blessing and it is safe to say they spoiled her.[31]

Intelligent and well educated, Fannie had a great love for art, literature, and finery. Claiming she did not care what anyone in town thought of her, Fannie actually enjoyed being the center of attention and her expensive taste in clothes always gave the older ladies of the parish something to gossip about. Ironically, it was often her honesty that led people to describe her as rebellious and willful. Following her conscience, instead of what was expected of her, she refused to become a full member of the church. Being the minister's daughter, this was a bold and difficult stand.

Chamberlain, the studious and religious farm boy from Brewer, was captivated by the lively, brown-eyed beauty who had a reputation for speaking her mind. He began escorting her to church and college socials, and their love blossomed.

Falling in love didn't seem to interfere with his studies. In his senior year at Bowdoin, Chamberlain won a prize for English composition. He was also selected to give a speech at his graduation ceremony. Unfortunately, he had to deliver it on the college's 50th anniversary which meant the First Parish Church where the commencement exercise was held, was packed, its galleries crowded with friends, families, learned professors, and former Bowdoin graduates representing, Joshua said, "all the dignitaries of the Nation." In the audience that day was the 14th President of the United States, Franklin Pierce, the famous poet Henry Wadsworth Longfellow, and the author of The Scarlet Letter and The House of the Seven Gables, Nathaniel Hawthorne. The tension proved to be too great. Standing on the stage in front of this distinguished audience, Joshua began his speech, and to his horror, he started to stutter. "For

Joshua L. Chamberlain   **Frances Caroline Adams Chamberlain**

a moment all around him swum and swayed in a mist," he said, and he almost fainted. Though the speech he had prepared so carefully was ruined, he managed to continue. Walking back and forth across the stage to keep from passing out, he recited those parts he could remember, his face burning with embarrassment. Of that humiliating experience Chamberlain further wrote: "The crestfallen champion was glad to get out of town."[32]

Getting out of town meant going to the Bangor Theological Seminary to study for the ministry. During the three years he was there, he and Fannie, who were engaged to be married, never saw each other. Fannie was living in Milledgeville, Georgia, teaching voice and piano at a private girl's school. Though time and distance separated them, their love was kept alive through romantic letters. Still, there were some doubts about marriage and a life together. In one letter to Joshua, Fannie writes that she is not cut out to be a minister's wife: "...my whole mind, character and temperament are entirely inappropriate for that position and I never could be useful in it."[33] Considering that Joshua was studying to be a minister, this must have troubled him. In a letter to her he writes: "I believe that God is over all things & that he will put me where he wants me and where I ought to be."[34]

It seems God wanted Joshua back at Bowdoin. A week after graduating from Bangor Theological Seminary, Chamberlain, who was also receiving his master's degree from Bowdoin, was asked to give another speech at the Bowdoin graduating ceremony. Back on the same stage where he had been humiliated three years before, he delivered a powerful speech entitled *Law and Liberty*. The professors in the audience were so impressed that Joshua was offered a job teaching at the college. Instead of becoming an ordained minister, Chamberlain became, to Fannie's relief, a college professor.[35]

John Calhoun Chamberlain   **Horace Beriah Chamberlain**

On The Road To War

"...I fear this war, so costly of blood and treasure, will not cease until the men of the North are willing to leave good positions, and sacrifice the dearest personal interests, to rescue our Country. . . . This war must be ended, with a swift and strong hand; and every man ought to come forward and ask to be placed at his proper post."

-Joshua L. Chamberlain in a letter to Maine's Governor,
Israel Washburn, July 14, 1862[36]

Sitting in the Chamberlain family's pew inside the First Parish Church in Brunswick, I was moved by the surrounding beauty and history. The dark woodwork that frames the network of Gothic arches and the intricate pattern of balcony railings lends a rich contrast to the light walls. The windows are stained glass, the floor carpeted, the pipes of its impressive organ ripple across the wall of the choir loft and stretch toward the ceiling like golden fingers.

Inside this church that radiates a spirit of communion, Harriet Beecher Stowe received the inspiration for Uncle Tom's Cabin, while attending Sunday service. It was here that Joshua Chamberlain conducted the choir, and gave his Bowdoin graduating speeches. It was here that he met Fannie, and where he would marry her on December 7, 1855.[37]

After returning from their honeymoon, the happy couple settled in Brunswick. While Joshua taught rhetoric and oratory at Bowdoin during the day, Fannie worked on her paintings and kept up the rooms they rented at the Stanwood house. In 1856, their first child was born. They named their baby daughter Grace, and the proud father called her "an angel of God."[38]

As Joshua settled into a life of teaching, marriage, and fatherhood, the first sparks of war were igniting across the country. From the deep south to the borders of Canada, Quakers, Christians, and abolitionists were helping slaves escape to freedom through a network known as the Underground Railroad. In Washington D.C., the heated debate over slavery touched off an ongoing political battle so intense that one northern senator was beaten right on the floor of the Senate by a cane-wielding southern congressman. Adding to the tempest was the Dred Scott vs. Sandford case, in which the Supreme Court ruled 6-3 that blacks were considered property;

that they had no rights of citizenship; and that Congress could not abolish slavery in a U.S. territory.[39]

Meanwhile, in Brunswick, Horace and John Chamberlain, like their brother before them, were students at Bowdoin. Horace graduated in 1857, John in 1859. Joshua, whose family had always been close, enjoyed having his younger brothers on campus, and the three spent a great deal of time together. The year Horace graduated and went on to become a lawyer, Joshua and Fannie's second child was born. The baby, described by his grandfather as "the image of Fannie," was born three months early and lived for only a few hours.[40] In October of the following year, their third child arrived. To his parents relief, Harold Wyllys Chamberlain, who would always be called Wyllys, was a healthy baby.

Grace Dupee Chamberlain

Harold Wyllys Chamberlain

In the spring of 1859, Joshua bought the Fales house where Henry Wadsworth Longfellow and his wife had lived years before. Chamberlain took pride in his new home, often getting up at dawn to work in the gardens before classes. Elsewhere in the country that year, northern congressmen in Washington were still trying to stop the spread of slavery in new states opening up in the west. Politicians representing the South believed the decision of whether these new states were free or slave should be made by the people who lived there, not by northern congressmen. Furthermore, because of the 1857 Supreme Court ruling that slaves were "property," southerners settling into these territories protested that the government had no right to tell them what they could or could not do with their "property." Adding to the tension, abolitionists staged their own protests, calling for the complete end of slavery in all states. One of these protesters, John Brown, would take this cause to the extreme. On the night of October 16, 1859, this abolitionist led a band of followers on a raid at Harpers Ferry, Virginia. The raid was intended to be the first step in a war against slavery and Brown, believing the slaves would rally to the cause once armed against their masters, brought along a wagon full of weapons: two hundred rifles, two hundred pistols, and a thousand pikes (spears). Although he managed to take control of several buildings, including the Federal arsenal, Brown's rebellion never happened. President Buchanan ordered in the Marines under the command of Colonel Robert E. Lee. Brown, and what was left of his army were captured. John Brown was tried, convicted of treason, and hanged on December 2, 1859.[41]

In 1860, Joshua and Fannie suffered the loss of another child. Emily Stelle Chamberlain's brief stay on earth only lasted from spring until September. Remembering his infant daughter, Chamberlain wrote that she "left but a summer smile and aching hearts, as she departed with the flowers."[42]

On November 6th of that same year, Abraham Lincoln was elected 16th President of the United States. Those living in the south regarded his election as a threat to their way of life and an end to their political power in Washington. Feeling they had no other choice, southern states began to secede. On December 20, 1860, South Carolina declared itself a free and independent state. In two months, the number of states leaving the Union would rise to seven. Representatives from South Carolina, Mississippi, Florida, Alabama, Georgia, and Texas met in Montgomery, Alabama and formed the Confederate States of America, electing Jefferson Davis as their president on February 9th, 1861.[43]

At four-thirty in the morning on April 12, 1861, the first shots of the war were fired at Fort Sumter, in Charleston Harbor, South Carolina. Thirty-four hours and about four-thousand shells later, Federal soldiers inside the fort surrendered to the Confederates. Amazingly, until this point no lives had been lost on either side. As a condition of their surrender, the Federals asked that they be allowed to give their flag a one-hundred-gun salute before leaving the fort. Tragically, while doing so, a cannon cartridge was ignited by sparks as it was being loaded. The explosion killed two soldiers and wounded four others. "In this pointless accident," wrote Swafford Johnson, "fell the first soldiers of the war."[44]

The Civil War, which would claim the lives of over 600,000 men, had begun. After President Lincoln asked for 75,000 volunteers to join the regular army, some of the upperclassmen at Bowdoin immediately enlisted. The patriotic fever quickly spread across the campus, and two drill companies were organized by the students: the Bowdoin Guard, and the Bowdoin Zouaves. One of Chamberlain's biographers humorously writes: "without uniforms, but armed with guns and ammunition furnished by the government, the students marched and skirmished down Maine Street...as if bent on capturing the Topsham bridge."[45]

It must have been difficult for Joshua to keep his mind on teaching during this time. It also must have been hard for him to say good-bye to his beloved students who had answered Lincoln's call. That year, on his sixth wedding anniversary, he found himself having to say good-bye to someone else he loved. Of his three younger brothers, Horace was the closest in age, and the most like him. Between them there had always been a special bond and Horace's death, from tuberculosis, was a crushing blow. As one would expect, Joshua had a difficult time accepting his brother's death. Often, he would think of something he wanted to tell Horace, only to remember that his brother was no longer there to tell. In a letter to his sister Sae, Joshua says how unfair it seemed that their brother "should be cut down at the very opening of his career" as a successful lawyer, and that his wife should be left a widow so young. He further told Sae that with Horace's death "one of the greatest sources of pleasure in this world was sealed up."[46]

Like Joshua, the country too, was sick at heart--already engaged in a bloody war that found brothers fighting against brothers, and fathers against sons. Putting aside his personal grief to recognize an even greater one, Joshua knew he could stand idle no longer. He firmly believed that the country his forefathers fought for should remain united and that it was his patriotic duty to protect and preserve that union despite the sacrifices it might cause his family. Without consulting his colleagues, parents, or even his wife, Joshua volunteered his services, requesting a commission from Maine's Governor Israel Washburn. Although Washburn offered to make Joshua a colonel, Chamberlain, though flattered, politely declined. Joshua felt that with his lack of military experience he should start at a lower rank and work his way up. Thus, receiving "his proper post" as lieutenant colonel of the 20th Regiment Maine Volunteer Infantry, Joshua L. Chamberlain began his journey down the road of war and into the pages of history.[47]

Part Two:
One Day's Crown of Fire

Gen. Adelbert Ames

The 20th Maine Infantry

"You were making history. The world has recorded for you more than you have written. The centuries to come will share and recognize the victory won here, with growing gratitude."

-Joshua Chamberlain
Dedication of the 20th Maine Monuments
Gettysburg, October, 1889

Although the sky had lightened to a dusky gray, the sun had not yet risen above the green, rolling hills of Gettysburg. On the south side of Little Round Top, I walked along the wooded and rocky crest, thankful for the peacefulness of that early hour when deer show themselves to unexpected visitors and the bluejay's shrill cry slices the quiet morning air.

Standing beside the monument dedicated to the men of the 20th Maine who had given their lives to hold this ground, I found it easier to picture the battle I had read of so often--easier to understand why it was vital "to hold this ground at all costs."[1]

During my journey through the battlefields of Gettysburg, I also saw a broader picture that included, among other places, McPherson Ridge, where the battle of Gettysburg began. It was here that Union General John Reynolds rushed to the support of the heavily outnumbered Federal Cavalry, urging his men on with, "Forward! For God's sake, Forward!" and gave up his life carrying out his own command.[2]

I walked along Seminary Ridge, where the Iron Brigade made a courageous but temporary stand; through the Peach Orchard and the Wheat Field, where Union troops were cut down by the thousands, where the 1st Minnesota lost 215 of its 262 men. I saw Culp's Hill, where one brigade of New Yorkers held off an entire Confederate division in four separate attacks and would later, with the aide of Major General Winfield S. Hancock's troops and some of the Iron Brigade, continue to hold that valuable position.[3]

I climbed the rocks of Devil's Den, visited the hallowed grounds of Spangler's Spring, East Cemetery Hill, and the vast open field across which Pickett charged. I stood beside the statue of Warren and studied the terrain, gaining an inkling of the urgency he must have felt upon realizing that the Round Tops where undefended. And it became clear to me that to place the credit of victory on one man, one regiment, or one battle, was impossible. Seeing the whole picture, I realized that victory was an honor shared by all who risked or gave their lives--by all

Union officers like Reynolds, Vincent, Warren, Buford, Hancock--by all soldiers dressed in blue who had done their job with valor during those three horrendous days of battle known as The Battle of Gettysburg.

With this new understanding, I saw the battle on Little Round Top differently. Instead of the glorified hero created by novel and Hollywood, I saw Joshua L. Chamberlain as another noble officer capable of doing his job under great pressure and against great odds.

In 1863, up on the ridge of the south side of Little Round Top, where the blood of the men from Maine lay in rocky pools that hot July afternoon, where the Alabama regiments charged, where the battle line moved back and forth like a wave through the smoke and rain of bullets, Chamberlain was at his proper post, as were the brave men of his regiment--defending, as ordered, the Union's left flank.

The 979 men of the 20th Maine came from all parts of the state: from the lumber camps of its pine forests, from the fishing villages of its rocky coast, from the fields of its central and western farms, and from rural towns in-between. In all, they came from ten counties, and because of that Chamberlain said, "It was not one of the state's favorites; no county claimed it; no city gave it a flag; and there was no send-off at the station."[4]

The men ranged in age between eighteen and forty-five, the average height was five feet, eight inches. Almost all had been born and raised in New England, and farming, lumbering, and fishing were the most common jobs left behind. Hardened by Maine winters and the physical work that came with felling trees, plowing fields, and hauling nets and traps, these men were, for the most part, hardy and well-built. Salted with the kind of independence that comes from living in the woods or on isolated farms, they were not used to taking orders from anyone but themselves and God. The man who was given the job to train and lead these men was Colonel Adelbert Ames, a graduate of West Point, who had been wounded in the First Battle of Bull Run. Ames, a Maine native from Rockland, had his work cut out for him. The regiment assigned to his command was untrained, undisciplined, and knew nothing about the military. As Ames put it, "This is a hell of a regiment!"[5]

But the men of the 20th did have two things in their favor: their ability to shoot, and, motivated by a sense of duty or adventure, their willingness to be there. Enlisting as volunteers, they had answered Lincoln's call for 300,000 more troops and considered themselves patriots going off to fight the Rebels for the nation's benefit. The army they would fight for was the Union Army, named for its purpose--the preservation of the union of the United States. To their enemies in the south, all men from the north were known as Yankees or Federals.

In the eyes of the Rebel soldier, the Yankees had invaded southern soil, and for some that was reason enough to fight. For others, like General Lee, who was against secession and had previously served in the regular United States Army, it was a matter of honor and allegiance to his home state of Virginia.   For the South in general, the purpose of the war was rooted in

An unidentified Union soldier from Maine, armed with an Enfield rifled musket.

secession, in the desire to gain its independence from a government it believed threatened its State and property rights, and jeopardized its livelihoods. Because the South was fighting to establish a confederacy of independent states (the Confederate States of America) their army was called the Confederate Army. To their enemies in the north they were known as Rebels or Confederates.

By the time the men of the 20th Maine arrived at Fort Mason (near Portland) to receive their basic training as Union soldiers, the war between the North and South was well underway. The odds were in the North's favor, and throughout the war its power would rest in population and industry. In the beginning, compared to the South, the North had 14 million more people, 92,000 more factories, and 18,600 more miles of railroad. It also had more financial resources. But at the onset of the war, the South had something the North lacked. It had Generals like Thomas J. Jackson, Pierre Beauregard, J.E.B. Stuart, Joseph Johnston, James Longstreet, and the brilliant Robert E. Lee. In the Eastern Theater during the first sixteen months of the war, the South's capable generals led their men to victories at the first and second Battle of Bull Run, Ball's Bluff, and during Jackson's stunning Shenandoah Valley campaign. Against a larger and better equipped army, the Rebels also managed to defeat the Yankees during the Seven Days' Battles of the Union's failed Peninsular Campaign.

Major victories for the North during this time were being won by its army in the West. In northern Tennessee, Fort Henry fell into Union hands on February 6, 1862. A week later, General Ulysses S. Grant bombarded Fort Donelson and, after delivering the famous message, "No terms except an immediate and unconditional surrender can be accepted," captured the fort and 15,000 Rebel soldiers. Two months later, Grant, who had once been forced to resign from the army in 1854 for excessive drinking, would win the bloody battle of Shiloh in southern Tennessee. Despite the heavy casualties of its troops at Shiloh, in the West, it seemed the North could do no wrong. By mid-summer of 1862, its army and navy had managed to capture Memphis, western Tennessee, New Orleans, Baton Rouge, and Natchez. Now, the only thing standing in the way of their complete control of the Mississippi River Valley was a place called Vicksburg. Still, the fact that the North was winning the war in the West took a back-seat to the fact that it was losing the war in its own front yard. The embarrassment of having been defeated in every major battle in Virginia had President Lincoln replacing one general after another in attempts to find one that could match skills with General Lee.[6]

After just a month of training at Fort Mason, the 20th Maine left for Washington on September 2, 1862. They rode the train out of Union Station in Portland to Boston, Massachusetts, then took the steamer *Merrimac* to Virginia. Prior to their arrival, the North had suffered another costly and humiliating defeat. For the second time at Bull Run, Lee's army, known as the Army of Northern Virginia, sent the Yankees running back to Washington. The *Merrimac* sailed into Alexandria, Virginia just in time for Joshua Chamberlain and his regiment to see boats returning with the wounded.

On September 7, 1862, the 20th Maine arrived in the Union's capitol. For men who came mostly from rural areas, the busy city of Washington must have been both exciting and a little unnerving. On their first night there, they slept in an empty lot close to the U.S. Arsenal. Ellis Spear, a company commander from Wiscasset, Maine, described it as "a downy bed of cats, bricks, and broken bottles."[7] That night, so far from home and so close to war, many thoughts must have turned to Maine and loved ones. For Chamberlain, it would mean thoughts of Fannie and his children. Little Grace, who he affectionately called Daisy, would be six in another month. Wyllys, who had his mother's dark hair and brown eyes, would be turning four. And Fannie, his wife, his friend, the mother of his children...their last night together had been spent in a wet tent at Fort Mason weathering a wild summer storm that verged on a hurricane.

Joshua also must have wondered how his brother Tom was doing. Because of a temporary illness, Tom, a sergeant in the 20th Maine, was unable to leave Fort Mason. At thirty-three, Joshua was almost thirteen years older than Tom, and the responsibility of watching out for his little brother must have weighed heavily on his mind. His father had instructed him to "Come home with honor" and "Take care of Tom," but for the time being the second order was out of Joshua's hands.[8]

The next day, carrying their new Enfield rifles, ammunition, and other gear, the 20th Maine headed out for Fort Craig. With only four weeks of training, the men still lacked basic military skills--like marching. Their efforts to keep in step during the seven-mile hike so embarrassed Colonel Ames that he told them, "If you can't do any better than you have tonight, you better all desert and go home!"[9]

The main Federal force in Virginia was the Army of the Potomac, named for the river upon whose banks the nation's capitol was built. Like Lee's Army of Northern Virginia, the Army of the Potomac was divided into corps. A corps was typically comprised of three divisions, a division of three brigades, and a brigade of four or more regiments. A regiment usually started out with about a thousand men. The 20th Maine was assigned to the Army of the Potomac's 5th Corps, 1st Division, 3rd Brigade. The 3rd Brigade, known as "Butterfield's Light Brigade" was made up of six regiments. They came from New York, Pennsylvania, Michigan and, with the new arrivals, Maine.[10]

At that time, the commander of the Army of the Potomac was General George B. McClellen, affectionately known to his men as "Little Mac." Although McClellen was a master at organizing and training an army, he had trouble utilizing it once the troops were in the field, as he had already proven during the Peninsular Campaign. "He lacked the skill to plan campaigns or handle large bodies of troops" said a soldier with the Army of the Potomac, who took part in every one of its major campaigns.[11] It was a weakness General Lee had already taken advantage of, and would again, in the very next battle. In September of 1862, Lee's Army of Northern Virginia was on the move. Crossing the Potomac River, Lee invaded Maryland. For the first time in the war, the South would fight on Northern soil. On September 12th, the 1st Division of the Fifth Corps, which included the 20th Maine, began their march toward South Mountain and Sharpsburg. They marched between sixteen and twenty-four miles

Thomas Davee Chamberlain

a day--quite an accomplishment for the green troops from Maine. The weather was hot and humid; the dusty roads were lined with equipment and personal items discarded by soldiers trying to lighten their loads. In a letter to his brother, Holman S. Melcher of the 20th Maine wrote, "I stood the march much better than I expected, and I have warm friends in the camp and regt., those who are ready to assist me in time of need, even Lt. Col. Chamberlain took my blankets onto his horse this forenoon."[12]

For the men of the 20th, any romantic ideas about the glory and adventure of war were put to rest as they marched along Turner's Gap through South Mountain. General John Gibbon's "Black Hat" brigade and the Confederates had fought there thirty-six hours before and the evidence of their struggle was heart-wrenching. Trees were riddled with bullets; the ground was littered with guns, hats, and bodies. In the midst of this carnage, a Rebel soldier, no older than sixteen, rested upright with his back against a tree. At first Chamberlain thought the boy, who held a small Bible in his hand, was sleeping. Upon closer inspection, he saw the blood-stained shirt. Later, he wrote, "this was my enemy--this boy! Oh, God forgive those who make us so!" It was an image that would continue to haunt him even nineteen years later when he recorded: "He was dead--the boy, my enemy; but I shall see him forever."[13]

On the 17th of September, the bloodiest single day of battle during the war was fought at Antietam Creek. The men of the 20th Maine were among the twenty-five thousand troops held in reserve and, although they did not fight that day, they witnessed some of the battle from a far-off ridge. The killing lasted from dawn until sunset: 23,500 casualties in all. Southern General A. P. Hill, rushing his division from Harpers Ferry to Sharpsburg (a distance of seventeen miles) arrived just in time to rescue Lee's troops and put an end to the day's battle.[14]

Lee's army had suffered tremendous losses, but his men stood their ground the next day, waiting for another fight that never came. That night, Lee slipped his army back across the Potomac.

McClellan's reluctance to use his reserve troops at Antietam brought him severe criticism, but his failure to fight on the 18th or to pursue Lee's retreating army while they were greatly outnumbered and in a weakened state, eventually cost him his command. For the unseasoned 20th Maine, McClellan's over-cautiousness was undoubtedly a blessing.

The 20th Maine's first encounter with the Rebels came two days later, during a much smaller confrontation. Because it was necessary to know how far Lee's army had retreated, several brigades, along with some cavalry, went on reconnaissance, the 20th Maine among them. After crossing the Potomac at Shepherdstown Ford, the brigades began climbing the high cliffs that led to flat ground above the river. Just as the 20th Maine began splashing into the water, they noticed that most of those who had gone before them were now scrambling back down the cliffs. As no retreat order had been given, the 20th kept moving forward. By the time they made it to the banks on the Virginia side of the river, however, the Union bugles on the Maryland side were sounding for retreat.

It was a confusing situation. From the top of the cliffs came the crackle of Confederate fire as Rebels took aim on the men crossing the river below. In an attempt to stop the Rebel fire, Union artillery on the opposite bank opened up with their cannons. The 20th Maine and other regiments were caught in the middle. Amidst the blast and boom of cannons, while bullets known as minie balls pelted the water, Chamberlain stopped his horse in a deep part of the river and calmly sat there, reassuring his men during their orderly retreat. He remained where he was until the horse he had borrowed that day was shot beneath him, forcing him to return to the Maryland banks.[15]

After this skirmish, the 20th would not engage in any real action until Fredericksburg. In the interim, they spent six weeks on the banks of the Potomac where, under the hard-driving command of Colonel Ames, they were drilled relentlessly. Ames was determined to turn the men into soldiers who were so well trained that in the heat of battle every action, from complex maneuvers to the nine steps it took to load and fire an Enfield, was automatic. As a combat veteran, Ames knew only too well what became of untrained men. He demanded obedience and perfected military skills from the 20th Maine, and although many of the men hated him at the time, later they would fully appreciate his unyielding discipline.

The relationship between Colonel Ames and Lieutenant Colonel Chamberlain was one of mutual respect and friendship. Chamberlain had proven himself a competent officer, one that Ames could rely on to get the job done right. The two shared a tent, and in the evenings Ames taught the eager professor the military tactics he had learned at West Point. The inner drive that had led Joshua to persistently study Greek and Latin in his parents' attic, was now focused on the subject of war.   He read every military manual he could find and asked questions of the more experienced officers in the camp. As he had once told Maine's Governor Washburn, "I have always been interested in military matters, and what I do not know in that line, *I know how to learn.*"[16]

Among the men, Joshua was highly respected.   One private went so far as to say, "Lieutenant Colonel Chamberlain is almost idolized by the whole regiment."[17] One reason might have been that he never put his own needs above those of his men. When it was necessary for them to sleep on the ground without a tent, so did he, even though as Lt. John Marshall Brown pointed out, "he had a whole regiment at his command to build him a shelter."[18] The college professor adapted easily to his job as an officer, and actually enjoyed it, telling Fannie in one letter that "no danger & no hardship ever makes me wish to get back to that college life again."[19] He thrived on a diet that included rationed meats, beans, and a mainstay of hardtack and coffee. Like his brother Tom, who had caught up with the regiment after recovering from his illness, Joshua had even gained some weight. Others were not as fortunate.

During the Civil War, more men died from disease than were killed in combat. The odds of a soldier dying of typhoid, dysentery, or pneumonia versus being killed on the battlefield were a staggering three to one. The soldiers of the 20th Maine were no exception. By the end of October, the regiment had been whittled down from 979 to 550 men. On the night of October 30, 1862, these remaining men left their Maryland camp and, with the rest of the 5th Corps, began marching south toward the Rappahannock River.[20]

Fredericksburg

The warm days of fall had come to an end, and a cold snap gave forewarning of a harsher season. Even greater changes were in the air. President Lincoln's forthcoming Emancipation Proclamation would bring to the Civil War a new and higher cause--a moral stand against slavery. For the Army of the Potomac there would also be a change of command. Having lost patience with General McClellan's reluctance to fight, President Lincoln replaced him with General Ambrose E. Burnside on November 5, 1862. Under Burnside, the Army of the Potomac was divided into three Grand Divisions (Right, Center, and Left) consisting of two corps each. The men of the 20th, now part of the Center Grand Division led by General "Fighting Joe" Hooker, were finally on the move and ready for battle.[21]

The plan was to make another attempt at capturing the Confederate capitol of Richmond. To do so, General Burnside proposed that the Army of the Potomac cross the Rappahannock River at Fredericksburg and, moving southward, force Lee into battle somewhere between Fredericksburg and Richmond before proceeding on to the Confederate capitol. Reluctantly, Lincoln approved the plan, warning General Burnside: "it will succeed, if you move very rapidly; otherwise not."[22] It was an accurate prediction.

When the Right Grand Division arrived on the banks opposite from Fredericksburg on November 17, 1862, the town was only occupied by a few Confederates. It was a perfect opportunity for the Union to overtake the town and secure the high ground, but almost immediately after their arrival, a bad storm struck, causing the Rappahannock River to rise. The Union's luck wasn't about to change. The pontoon boats, which were used to both ferry troops and fashion bridges, had been somehow waylaid. A fortnight was lost, and in the interim, General Lee secured Fredericksburg with both Longstreet and Jackson's troops. By the time Burnside finally attacked with his Grand Divisions thirteen days later, the Confederates had the high ground of Fredericksburg so well fortified that the Union soldiers would find themselves marching into, as Chamberlain put it, "a death trap."[23]

About ten o'clock on December 13th, after the heavy morning fog lifted from the Rappahannock River, the slaughter began. On the outskirts of Fredericksburg toward Hamilton's Crossing, the Union's Left Grand Division tried to turn Lee's right flank and was forced to retreat. Meanwhile, the heaviest fighting would occur at Marye's Heights, where, by nightfall, 9,000 Union soldiers would be killed or wounded.[24]

Behind the protection of a solid stone wall that ran along a sunken road, Confederate riflemen were entrenched four men deep. Further back, strategically placed on the incline of

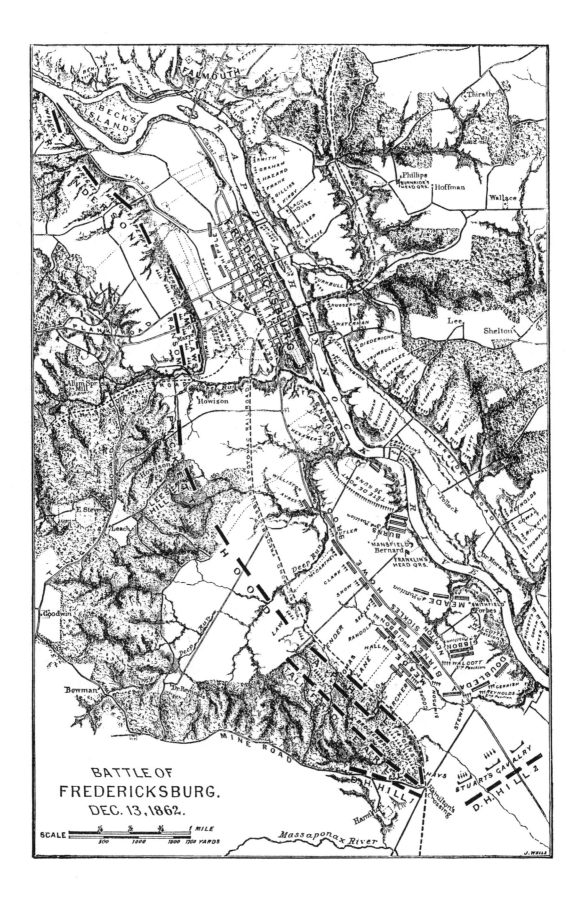

BATTLE OF
FREDERICKSBURG.
DEC. 13, 1862.

Marye's Heights, were their cannons. In front of them was an open field. When General Longstreet questioned the strength of their position, his artillery chief told him, "A chicken could not live on that field when we open on it."[25] It was across that field that waves of Union troops charged courageously in a hopeless attempt to break through the Confederate line. Waiting their turn, the 20th Maine watched as the Right Grand Division made five unsuccessful charges, the men of the 2nd and 9th Corps falling in piles before what Chamberlain called, "the death-delivering stone wall." Instead of putting all the Union troops in at the same time, which would have given them a better chance of breaking through that Confederate wall, their generals led them to slaughter by brigades. By the time the 20th Maine was called upon, the field was blanketed with bodies.   Chamberlain writes:

> We picked our way amid bodies thickly strewn. . . .On we pushed, up slopes slippery with blood, miry with repeated, unavailing thread. We reached that final crest, before that all-commanding, countermanding stone wall. Here we exchanged fierce volleys at every disadvantage, until the muzzle-flame deepened the sunset red, and all was dark.[26]

That night, under cover of darkness, Joshua and his adjutant John Brown roamed the field together doing what they could for their suffering comrades. They scavenged canteens from the dead and gave them to the thirsty wounded, applied what little first aid they knew, and took note of last farewells from dying soldiers to their loved ones back home. Joshua said as they "advanced over that stricken field," a monotone of death whispered, "some breathing inarticulate agony; some dear home names; some begging for a drop of water; some for a caring word; some praying God for strength to bear; some for life; some for quick death."[27]

"Within pistol shot of the enemy," the 20th Maine slept among the dead.[28] It was cold, and with no overcoat to break the wind, Joshua sought shelter between two dead bodies. He used a third body for a pillow, and, to protect his face from the bone-chilling breeze, he covered it with the flap of the dead man's coat. "All night the winds roared," he said, and in the wind-blown rhythm of a loosened window shutter, he imagined that he heard the haunting refrain, "Never-forever; forever-never!"[29]

The next morning, the 14th of December, Chamberlain said he was:

> wakened by the sharp fire that spoke the dawn, as I lifted my head from its restful though strange pillow, there fell out from the breast pocket a much-worn little New Testament written in it the owner's name and home. I could do no less than take this to my keeping, resolved that it should be sent to that home in the sweet valley of the Susquehanna as a token that he who bore it had kept the faith and fought the fight.[30]

That day, trapped by the fire of the stone wall and unable to advance or retreat, the 20th Maine remained on the field where survival meant using dead bodies for protection against cross-fire.

The City of Fredericksburg along the Rappahannock River.

When darkness came, Joshua said they buried their dead "in the earth they had made dear." They used bayonets and shell fragments to dig the shallow graves; headstones were "broken fencerails or musket-butts" into which they "rudely carved under sheltered match-light...each name and home."[31] As if ordered by the dead or God, the aurora borealis appeared in the sky that night, and Chamberlain thought it a "befitting scene!...Dead for their country's honor, and lighted to burial by the meteor splendors of their Northern home!"[32]

Ordered to withdraw, the 20th retreated back to the town of Fredericksburg, where they spent the rest of that night and the following day. At nightfall on the 15th, the 20th Maine and two other regiments were ordered back into the field. There, soldiers of the 20th began digging trenches so close to the enemy line that they could hear the Rebel voices. At one point, Chamberlain, who was checking the position of his line in the dark, ventured a little too far. Mistaking a Rebel soldier for one of his own, he told him, "Throw to the other side, my man; that's where the danger is!" "Golly!" said the soldier, "Don't ye s'pose I know which side them Yanks be? They're right onto us now." Chamberlain, who could speak nine languages put his ability to imitate accents to use. Pretending to be a Confederate officer he ordered, "Dig away then, but keep a right sharp lookout!"[33]

Unknown to the Union regiments that were digging rifle pits which would never be used, the rest of the Army of the Potomac had retreated back across the Rappahannock River. When a staff officer finally arrived to tell them, "Get yourselves out of this quick as God will let you! The whole army is across the river!" he said it so loudly that it was easily overheard by the Rebel line. Chamberlain, ever quick on his feet, ordered back in an even louder voice, "Steady in your places, my men! One or two of you arrest this stampeder! This is a ruse of the enemy! We'll give it to them in the morning!"[34]

Although the trick worked, the regiments still had the difficult task of retreating across the field. To avoid suspicion, Chamberlain said they withdrew slowly, every odd and even man moving back at different intervals, a hundred or so yards at a time. This harrowing procedure, the retreat through the deserted town of Fredericksburg, and the crossing of the Rappahannock River--would take the rest of the night.

The next morning, as the exhausted men rested on the Union side of the river, General Hooker rode up to them. "You've had a hard chance, Colonel," he said to Chamberlain. "I'm glad to see you out of it!"

"It was chance, General," said Joshua, then as if to sum up the whole three days of battle, he added, "not much intelligent design there!"

Hooker quickly defended himself, "God knows I did not put you in!"

Chamberlain, tired, angry, and disgusted by the string of blunders that cost the lives of so many brave men, shot back, "That was the trouble, General. You should have put us in. We were handled in piecemeal, on toasting-forks."[35] Although it was a risky thing to say to a superior officer, Chamberlain was right, and "Fighting Joe" Hooker did not reprimand him.

Despite being outnumbered by 43,500 men, General Lee's Army of Northern Virginia had won again. Lee had easily anticipated General Burnside's plans, and with ample time to consolidate his troops and fortify the high ground, his army was able to present a masterful defense. Of the Union's defeat, one Northern correspondent wrote, "It can hardly be in human nature for men to show more valor, or generals to manifest less judgement."[36]

After the battle of Fredericksburg, the defeated Army of the Potomac returned to Falmouth, Virginia, where they built their winter camps. In mid-January of 1863, General Burnside attempted another campaign on Fredericksburg, but the heavy winter rains and a recent thaw turned his idea and the roads to mud. "Men, horses, artillery, pontoons, and waggons were stuck in the mud," said Lieutenant Elisha Hunt Rhodes of Company D, 2nd Rhode Island Volunteers. He said the mud was so deep that mules and horses actually drowned in it, and that Rebels on the opposite bank made mocking signs that read, "Burnside stuck in the mud."[37] After four days of sloshing his army through the mire, Burnside called an end to the campaign, and when the "Mud March" was over, so was General Burnside's command of the Army of the Potomac.

In February of 1863, Joshua was granted leave and returned to Maine to visit both his family and the state's new governor, Abner Coburn. The 20th Maine needed officers to help fill the vacancies in the regiment, and Joshua asked Coburn for help. After Fredericksburg and living in winter quarters, being back in Brunswick with his loving family must have been a welcomed change. In his absence, Joshua had missed birthdays, Thanksgiving, Christmas, and even more, the day-to-day life with his growing children. His leave provided him just a few precious days to make up for it.[38]

When Joshua returned to his regiment, "Fighting Joe" Hooker was the new commander of the Army of the Potomac. Under Hooker, the morale of the men and the living conditions in winter quarters had greatly improved. Hooker provided the soldiers with better food, new equipment, new uniforms; he enforced stricter sanitary conditions and military drilling. Maintaining the corps structure, he did away with the three Grand Divisions and reorganized his cavalry.[39]

By April, the Army of the Potomac was gearing up for a new campaign to capture Richmond. General McClellan's Peninsular Campaign on Richmond had been from the east; his replacement, Burnside, had tried it from the north; and Burnside's replacement, Hooker, would make a sweep to his right and try it from the west. Hooker's sweep involved marching twenty-five miles up the Rappahannock, crossing that river and its tributary, the Rapidan, at Germanna and Ely's fords, then marching down the south bank through the Wilderness. As one soldier humorously put it, "The army commenced its annual movement toward Richmond, this time its route by way of Chancellorsville."[40]

On April 27, 1863, the Army of the Potomac left camp on its newest campaign. Hooker, whose optimism President Lincoln did not fully trust, was quoted as saying, "May God have mercy on General Lee, for I will have none."[41] Much to their disappointment, the soldiers of the 20th Maine would not be going along. A number of men in the regiment had been inoculated with a faulty vaccine, resulting in an outbreak of over eighty cases of smallpox and several deaths. Although Chamberlain requested a temporary place on another general's staff so he would not be left out of the fight, the request was denied. Instead, he found himself in charge of the quarantined outfit, replacing Colonel Ames who had somehow managed to secure himself a place on General Meade's staff.

Hooker's plan was a simple one and he had 115,000 men to make it work. To hold Lee's attention at Fredericksburg, he kept a third of his army there, the rest made the sweep, marching with speed toward the unprotected rear of Lee's army. If Hooker outflanked Lee, it would force a Confederate retreat, allowing Hooker to choose the ground for the next battle en route to Richmond. Thus, Hooker's goal was to flush out Lee's entrenched army and force them to battle on open ground where sheer Union numbers would determine victory. Although Hooker was able to smoothly carry out the first part of his plan, maneuvering 70,000 of his men to Chancellorsville, the uncanny Lee, alerted to the danger in his rear, was already making moves of his own.

Ignoring all of Hooker's diversions, Lee left a skeleton force of 10,000 men at the well fortified Fredericksburg to contend with the Union troops there, then he took his remaining 45,000 men to Chancellorsville to meet Hooker head on, crossing the Rapidan on the night of April 29th. On May 1st, Hooker's army began moving but quickly and unexpectedly ran into Confederate opposition. To Hooker's surprise, Lee's rear had suddenly become his front. The shock of that discovery caused Hooker to loose confidence in himself and he retreated back to Chancellorsville. Now facing a force of 70,000 men against his 45,000, Lee gave Hooker another surprise--in the presence of an enemy force larger than his own, Lee divided his army, sending 26,000 men with Stonewall Jackson on a fourteen-mile hike through the woods to hit Hooker's unprotected right flank. At six o'clock on May 2nd, while the Union troops were making supper, Stonewall Jackson's men stormed out of the woods in a mile-wide attack and shattered Hooker's right flank.[42]

From "Quarantine Hill," Chamberlain heard the steady boom of distant cannons. Desperately wanting to get in the fight, he rode over to General Butterfield's headquarters and begged the General to let the 20th Maine have any part in the battle. Upset that the request was denied, Chamberlain angrily pointed out, "if we couldn't do anything else we could give the rebels the small pox!"[43]

Perhaps impressed with Joshua's desire to fight or at least be useful, the next morning the 20th received orders to guard the Union's telegraph line that ran from Falmouth to Hooker's headquarters. While conducting this duty, Chamberlain, with one eye on the telegraph line and the other watching for some action, came across a perfect opportunity to get into the fray. On May 4th, he crossed the Rappahannock and joined General Charles Griffin's 1st Division of the 5th Corps in an attack against General J.E.B. Stuart, who was leading Stonewall Jackson's men. While rallying some troops, Chamberlain had another horse shot from under him.[44]

On May 5th, General Hooker, who had lost 17,000 men, ordered a complete withdrawal of

Union troops. When news of the battle reached Lincoln, he said, "My God! My God! What will the country say?"[45] Although General Lee had won a stunning victory at Chancellorsville, he had lost his most dependable, and one of the South's greatest generals. Stonewall Jackson had been shot by his own men when they mistook him for the enemy, and died eight days later of pneumonia.

When the defeated Army of the Potomac retreated back to their old camp, the 5th Corps acted as rearguard. A heavy rain had caused the river to rise, and the pontoon bridges were unstable. Chamberlain spent two days "at the bridges, which threatened to give way in the freshet, steadying the men by his presence and his calm words."[46]

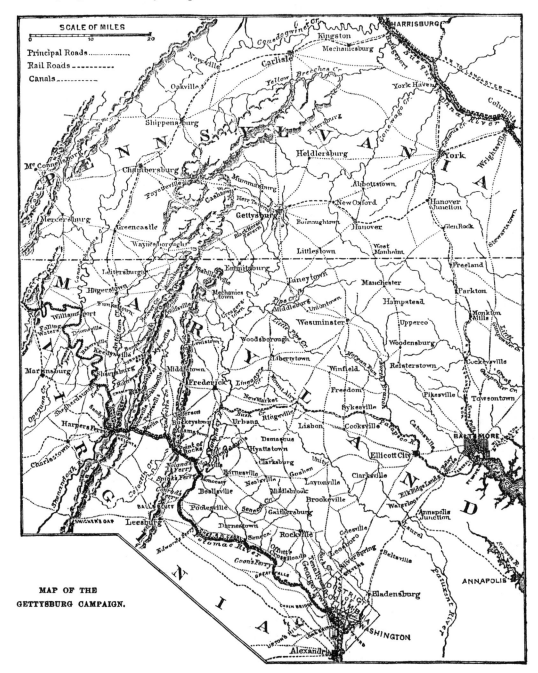

MAP OF THE
GETTYSBURG CAMPAIGN.

Gettysburg

A few weeks after the Battle of Chancellorsville, Colonel Ames was promoted to brigadier general and took command of a brigade in the 11th Corps. With recommendations by Ames and General Griffin, Joshua was promoted to colonel of the 20th Maine. Lt. John Brown followed Ames to the 11th Corps; in his place, Lt. Thomas Chamberlain became the regiment's acting adjutant, thus giving Tom a place on his brother's staff. One of Chamberlain's first challenges as Colonel was given to him by General Meade, who ordered Joshua to deal with some rebellious soldiers. The men of the 2nd Maine Regiment had been in the war since it began. Their two-year enlistment was now over, and most had headed back to Maine. Left behind were 120 of its soldiers who, under unfortunate circumstances, had signed papers for a three-year stint instead of two. Feeling they had been deceived by the recruiting officer and that their claims had been disregarded by the army they had fought so hard for, these men went on strike, refusing to do their duties or obey orders. These seasoned veterans were marched under guard to Chamberlain with orders from General Meade, the 5th Corps commander, to "make them do duty, or shoot them down the moment they refused."[47]

Chamberlain knew this was one order he could never carry out. These men were from Maine, most had grown up in the backyard of Bangor, just across the river from Joshua's boyhood home. As soldiers they had proven themselves in eleven battles and numerous skirmishes and had established a reputation as excellent fighters. Joshua also knew that if he didn't carry out Meade's order, the general would replace him with someone who would. Believing the delegated responsibility gave him "some discretionary power" he handled the situation his own way. So that the men from the 2nd Maine would no longer feel like prisoners, he dismissed the soldiers Meade had sent to guard them. He then ordered that their names be added to the rolls, assigning them to different companies within the regiment, knowing if he broke them up it would help to quell further disobedience. After they had eaten their first meal in three days, he gathered them together and talked to them:

> I had called them together and pointed out to them the situation: that they could not be entertained as civilian guests by me; that they were by authority of the United States on my rolls as soldiers, and I should treat them as soldiers should be treated; that they should lose no rights by obeying orders, and I would see what could be done for their claim.[48]

Joshua's promised efforts to defend their claim failed to bring results, but by treating the men of the 2nd Maine with deserved respect, honesty, and fairness, he had not only accomplished a difficult task but had also secured a new force of experienced men for his regiment--men whose skill and valor would help decide a battle near a little town called Gettysburg.

"To open the Mississippi River would be better than the capture of forty Richmonds," General Halleck told President Lincoln--and the city of Vicksburg was the key to that success.[49] After four failed attempts, the Union army in the West, under the command of General Grant, finally had Vicksburg under siege, and the focus of the war again turned to the armies of the Potomac and Northern Virginia. By June of 1863, both armies were on the move. In an effort to take the pressure off Vicksburg, as well as provide his home state of Virginia some needed relief from warfare, General Lee had invaded the North for the second time and was moving his troops toward Harrisburg, Pennsylvania with intentions of capturing the city. Isolated from his cavalry, which was operating too far east, Lee had no idea where the enemy was until a spy named Harrison told him they were right on his flank. In light of this information, Lee abandoned his plan to capture Harrisburg, deciding instead to establish a battle position near Cashtown where he could engage the enemy while threatening both Washington and Baltimore. Because Gettysburg provided strategic crossroads where he could first concentrate his troops, Lee headed his army there, converging on the town from the north.[50]

General George Meade, who had just replaced General Hooker as commander of the Army of the Potomac, had the same idea. To consolidate his troops, Meade pushed toward the town of Gettysburg from the south, intending to establish a battle position fifteen miles away at Big Pipe's Creek. Thus, the greatest battle in American history came about by chance and would be waged against the backdrop of green rolling hills and scenic farmland surrounding a town of 2,400 residents. It began on July 1st, 1863, and by the time it was over three days later, 51,000 men were dead, wounded, or missing-in-action.[51]

On the morning of July 1st, a Rebel division of Harry Heth's men headed toward Gettysburg to find a supply of shoes that were rumored to be in town. Already in the area and expecting trouble, were two brigades of Union cavalry commanded by John Buford. When the enemies crossed paths, the Battle of Gettysburg began. The fighting broke out on McPherson Ridge about eight o'clock in the morning. Although Buford's dismounted cavalry were outnumbered, they had one advantage--repeating rifles. These seven-shot Spencer carbines could fire twenty rounds a minute; the muzzle-loading Rebels could only fire three rounds in that same amount of time. "Buford's repeaters could be loaded on Monday and fired all week," the Rebels later said.[52]

Despite their thin line, Buford's men managed to hang on, delaying the Rebels for several hours until reinforcements arrived. After racing his 1st Corps to the field, General John Reynolds, one of the best commanders in the Union Army, was killed by a Rebel sharpshooter. Having expected only a small contingent of local militia and some cavalry to be in the area, the Rebels soon realized what kind of force they were dealing with when the legendary Black Hat Brigade slammed into the Confederate's flank: "Here are those damned black-hat fellers agin," the Rebels shouted, "Tain't no militia--that's the Army of the Potomac!"[53] The fighting increased throughout the day as reinforcements from both armies reached the field. By afternoon, Rebel troops had the outnumbered Yankees on the run, driving Union forces back to Cemetery Hill, south of town.

Although the Army of Northern Virginia won the first day of battle, Southern General Richard S. Ewell made a decisive mistake when he chose not to pursue the outnumbered Yankees on Cemetery Hill and Culp's Hill. Under the capable hands of Union General Winfield Scott Hancock, this area was well fortified during the night. Because of Hancock's foresight and ingenuity, by the next day, General Meade, whose troops were still arriving, was able to establish a strong defensive line shaped like a fish hook. Beginning at Culp's Hill, the fish hook curved around Cemetery Hill, its shank running along Cemetery Ridge and ending at the Round Tops. One mile away, on Seminary Ridge, which ran parallel to the Union's line, were Lee's men. Between the two ridges would soon be a vale of destruction.[54]

The woods on Little Round Top where the 20th Maine fought.

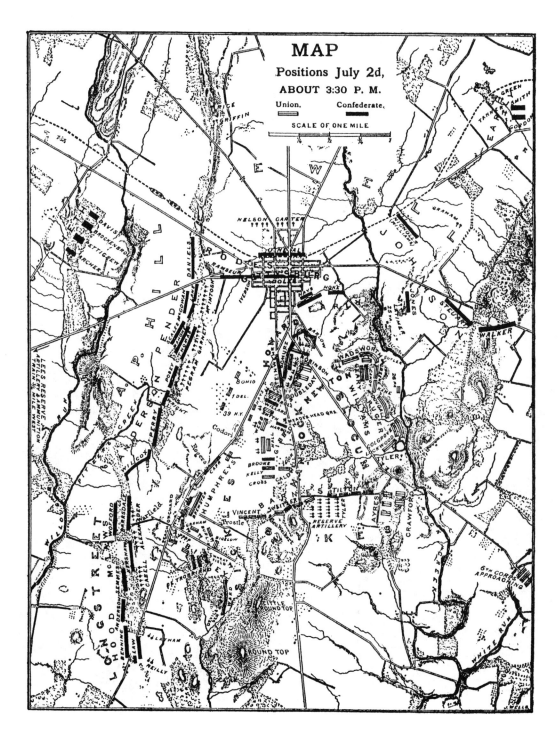

MAP
Positions July 2d,
ABOUT 3:30 P. M.

The night before, while Hancock's men were digging into the hills of the high ground, and while General Lee was still wondering where J.E.B. Stuart and his cavalry were, Chamberlain and the 20th Maine were marching. By the time they reached the heights east of Gettysburg on the morning of July 2nd, the exhausted men had marched a total of sixty-seven miles in three days. Accompanying the 20th Maine was John Chamberlain. John had caught up with Joshua and Tom on the 22nd of June, the day after the Middleburg skirmish. Having been educated and trained for the ministry at Bangor Theological Seminary, John worked for the Christian Commission, an organization whose volunteers "tended to the physical and spiritual needs of the soldiers and sailors."[55] Although Joshua enjoyed having John along, he now had one more brother to worry about in the approaching battle.

On that second day of battle, General Lee's plan for attack was to strike both of Meade's flanks. General Longstreet would assault the Union's left, and when General Ewell heard Longstreet's guns, he was to attack the Union's right. It was a good plan, but preparations were difficult. Without Stuart and his cavalry, Lee could not be sure of the size of the Union's force or how far their line extended. To gather this information, Captain S.R. Johnston was sent out on reconnaissance. The information that he gave Lee about the Round Tops was accurate--but by the time Longstreet was able to get his troops into position, changes had been made in the Union's line.[56]

General Lee, knowing Meade from the old army, said, "General Meade will commit no blunder on my front."[57] But as the curtain of battle was about to be lifted, Meade recognized a great blunder that could cost the Union army many lives and jeopardize its defensive position. The person responsible for this blunder was Union General Daniel E. Sickles. Sickles, whose 3rd Corps was situated along the southern part of Cemetery Ridge that held the Union's left flank, had decided, without orders, to move his men forward by a half a mile or more and establish a line from the Peach Orchard, through the Wheat Field, to Devil's Den. By doing this, Sickles put his men in a position so far ahead of the rest of the army, that it not only isolated them from the Union's line, but left the Round Tops unoccupied. In fact, it left him unsupported on both ends, and thinned his line by increasing the area he had to cover. As some soldiers put it, Sickels "stuck out like a sore thumb."[58] But there was nothing General Meade could do about it, Confederate shells were already falling. When Sickles offered to withdraw his troops, Meade, knowing it was too late, said, "The enemy will not allow you."[59] Almost immediately, from the Peach Orchard and the Wheat Field, came the shrill sound of Rebel yells as the fighting broke out in earnest.

Meanwhile, General Gouverneur K. Warren, sent by Meade to assess conditions on the extreme left, arrived at the summit of Little Round Top and was shocked to find only a handful of Union signalmen. Warren, Meade's chief engineer, was already familiar with the ground and capably sized up the situation. He would later write:

I saw that this was the key of the whole position and that our troops in the woods in front of it could not see the ground in front of them, so that the enemy would come upon them before they would be aware of it. The long line of woods on the west side of the Emmittsburg road, which was along a ridge, furnished an excellent place for the enemy to form out of sight, so I requested the Captain of a rifle battery just in front of Little Round Top to fire a shot into these woods. He did so, and as the shot went whistling through the air the sound of it reached the enemies' troops and caused every one to look in the direction of it. The motion revealed to me the glistening of gun barrels and bayonets of the enemy's line of battle already formed and far outflanking the position of any of our troops, so that the line of his advance from his right to Little Round Top was unopposed.[60]

Warren also knew if the Confederates were able to take possession of Little Round Top, they'd advance along Cemetery Ridge, rolling up the Union line like a rug. Thus, the race to occupy Little Round Top began. Warren sent word to Meade, then sought help from General Sykes, commander of the 5th Corps. Sykes immediately sent an aide to find his 1st Division commander General James Barnes with orders to get a brigade up to Little Round Top. In all the confusion, the aide was unable to locate Barnes, but luck was on the Union's side. Colonel Strong Vincent, commander of the 5th Corps, 3rd Brigade, intercepted the orders, and by his own authority, rushed his brigade, which included the 20th Maine, to the Union's rescue.[61]

"Under the storm of shells from Longstreet's batteries across the valley," Vincent's Brigade crossed Plum Run and scaled the craggy northern face of Little Round Top.[62] Chamberlain writes: "At that fiery moment three brothers of us were riding abreast, and a solid shot driving close past our faces disturbed me. 'Boys,' I said, 'I don't like this. Another such shot might make it hard for mother.'" He then ordered Tom, "go to the rear of the regiment, and see that it is well closed up!" Then he told John to "pass up ahead and look out a place for our wounded."[63]

Shortly before Warren discovered that Little Round Top was undefended, on the south side of Big Round Top, Confederate Colonel William Oates and his troops were in the process of sweeping the mountain clean of Union sharpshooters who had been giving Law's right flank trouble. Since three o'clock that morning, Oates' men, the 15th Alabama Regiment, plus the 47th Alabama, which was temporarily under his command, had marched a total of twenty-eight miles. The scramble up Big Round Top had been difficult, and at the 664 foot summit Colonel Oates gave his weary and thirsty men a rest. From the heights of this mountain, Oates surveyed the Union's line below, concluding that if his army could get some artillery where he was standing they could blow apart the Yankee line along Cemetery Ridge. As these thoughts were going through his mind, Captain Terrell of Law's Brigade rode up and informed Col. Oates that

The 20th Maine monument on Little Round Top.

General Law's orders were to "press forward." That meant leaving the advantage of the greater heights for the lesser ones below. Looking down at the 548 foot summit of Little Round Top, Oates saw that it was unmanned except for a few signalmen. Although he wanted his men to hold their position on Big Round Top, there were no generals in the area close enough to grant his request, and he could not waste time trying to track one down. Reluctantly, he let go of that moment of clear victory, and getting his men to their feet, began to descend the wooded and rocky mountain.[64]

Meanwhile, Vincent's 3rd Brigade was racing for the south side of Little Round Top where they made a quarter circle around and below the mountain's crest. Beginning on its right, the line consisted of the 16th Michigan, the 44th New York, the 83rd Pennsylvania, and the anchor of the Union's left flank--the 20th Maine. "I place you here!" Vincent told Chamberlain. "This is the left of the Union Line. You understand. You are to hold this ground at all costs!"[65]

Separating the two Round Tops was a narrow, wooded valley whose trees thinned out against the rocky slopes of Little Round Top. To protect his regiment's own left, Chamberlain dispatched Captain Morrill's Company B to his left and front as skirmishers. As the men of Morrill's company, who had a reputation as excellent marksmen, headed into the forested area to the left, Chamberlain turned his attention to preparing the rest of his regiment. Without Company B, he now had slightly over three hundred armed men, plus twenty-seven officers--he knew he needed more than that to hold the Union's flank. Chamberlain was not the only one who understood the crisis at hand. Without being ordered, the sick and injured soldiers in the rear came forward and went into the ranks. Joshua said, "even cooks and servants not liable to such service, asked to go in." Chamberlain also released the remaining handful of 2nd Maine mutineers from their guards, offering them the opportunity to fight, and he said "all but one or two" returned "manfully to duty."[66]

The line grew taut with expectation as the soldiers from Maine awaited the enemy. The shells had stopped falling behind them--a sure sign that the Confederate infantry was ready to strike. Through the eerie quiet, Chamberlain paced up and down the line, giving his men and officers words of encouragement. The air was humid, the temperature in the high eighties. The wait for battle was short by the clock and long by the nerves. Ten minutes. The Confederate attack was made by Law's Brigade (Hood's Division, Longstreet's Corps) plus the 4th and 5th Texas Regiments. Chamberlain writes:

> In a minute more came the roll of musketry. It struck the exposed right center of our brigade. Promptly answered, repulsed, and renewed again and again, it soon reached us, still extending. Two brigades of Hood's Division had attacked--Texas and Alabama. The Fourth Alabama reached our right, the Forty-seventh Alabama joined and crowded in, but gradually, owing to their echelon advance. Soon seven companies of this regiment were in our front. We had all we could stand. My attention was sharply called, now here, now there. In the thick and smoke, Lieutenant Nichols, a bright officer near our center, ran up to tell me something queer was going on in his front, behind those engaging us.[67]

To get a better view, Joshua climbed up on a large rock. From there, he saw a large force of Rebels working their way through the woods toward his front and extending beyond his left flank. Unknown to Chamberlain, the force he was about to engage was Colonel Oates and his 15th Alabama Regiment, which had just descended Big Round Top. Already anticipating what would happen, Chamberlain quickly improvised a defensive plan. While still firing at the enemy in the front, he had his men extend their line by falling into a single, rather than double, rank. This meant that after each man fired his gun, he took a few steps to the left, so the man in back of him could fall in beside him. Though this weakened the depth of the line, it doubled its length. Then, on the extreme left of Little Round Top, where the hill begins to curve, he planted the colors by a big boulder. His line from this point on was bent into a right angle. By doing this, the left wing of the 20th would meet the flanking enemy head on. The whole process was a difficult maneuver, especially under fire, but Chamberlain's men accomplished it in good order and without the enemy detecting the move. About his men's ability to execute this maneuver Chamberlain said, "Of rare quality were my officers and men. I shall never cease to admire and honor them for what they did in this desperate crisis."[68]

Colonel Oates, who first encountered the 20th Maine from their front and described the meeting as "the most destructive fire I ever saw," would soon swing his men toward the Union's extreme left in hope of dislodging the enemy from its rocky position.[69] But the solid Maine line that formed the angle and faced the flankers, came as a great surprise to Colonel Oates and his 15th Alabama Regiment. When the Rebels made their first assault from this direction, "the Maine men rose above the rocks and a volley flashed out that lighted all the fires of hell in that hot, shadowed backyard of the battle."[70] "The fire was so destructive," wrote Oates, "that my line wavered like a man trying to walk against a strong wind."[71] But, outnumbering the Maine men, the 15th Alabama made charge after charge. The 20th's angled line was getting hit from both the front and the side: "the air seemed to be alive with lead" said Theodore Gerrish of the 20th Maine, and "the line at times were so near each other that the hostile gun barrels almost touched."[72] "The edge of the conflict swayed to and fro, with wild whirlpools and eddies," said Chamberlain, "at times I saw around me more of the enemy than of my own men."[73]

Amid the carnage, Chamberlain also saw acts of courage. He said he had sent one young soldier, who had been wounded in the head, back to the hospital where the man could "at least die in peace." Thirty minutes later, during a "desperate rally," Chamberlain spotted the "noble youth," head covered with a bloody bandage, "in the thick of the fight."[74] Another time, after the center of his line was completely shot away, he saw Color-Sergeant Andrew Tozier firing a rifle while still holding up the staff of the flag. Using guns they had recovered from their fallen comrades, the only two remaining color guards gallantly tried to defend the entire gap in the center. To their aide, Joshua sent his brother Tom.[75]

A temporary lull in the action, gave way to a moment of justice. Previously, back in winter camp at Stoneman's Switch, Sergeant George Washington Buck had been unjustly reduced to private for refusing to cut a "bullying" quartermaster's personal firewood while Buck was ill.

A GROUP of MAINE PILGRIMS VISITING THE BATTLEFIELDS OF THE NATION;
LITTLE ROUND TOP, GETTYSBURG - PENNSYLVANIA, OCT. 2ⁿᵈ 1889.

0 MISS BEAL, 1 GENᴸ GEORGE L. BEAL, 2 GENᴸ J. L. CHAMBERLAIN, 3 GENᴸ S. H. MANNING,
4. BRONZE STATUE of GENᴸ WARREN.

(Above) Gen. Chamberlain and Maine veterans returning to Little Round Top in 1889. (Below) Dedication of the 20th Maine monument on Oct. 3, 1889.

This act of injustice toward a soldier who had fought so bravely at Fredericksburg had not escaped Chamberlain's notice. Finding Buck dying of a chest wound, Chamberlain righted that wrong. After Buck whispered, "Tell my mother I did not die a coward!" Chamberlain answered, "You die a sergeant. I promote you for faithful service and noble courage on the field of Gettysburg!"[76] Aware that his colonel would follow through with that promise, Buck died knowing his reputation as a soldier had been justly redeemed, and that, as a result, his mother would be placed on the rolls of the Country's benefactors.

While Chamberlain and the 20th engaged the left, to their right the fighting was also heavy. At the other end of the brigade's line, the 4th and 5th Texas slammed into the 16th Michigan, causing them to fall back. Confusion ensued, but Colonel Strong Vincent managed to rally his troops. "Don't yield an inch now, men, or all is lost!" he ordered, then he rushed in among the broken companies.[77] Vincent, who had taken it upon himself to answer Warren's call, and who had capably placed his brigade along this rocky slope, had just given his last command. A moment later, he was mortally wounded.

With Vincent no longer there to rally his men, the attacking Rebels were quickly gaining ground. But to everyone's surprise, the 140th New York arrived at a dead run, dashing into the fray without stopping to load their guns or form a line. Led by their gallant young colonel Patrick O'Rorke, Chamberlain said this regiment would help save the Union's line "in that moment of threatened doom."[78] O'Rorke, who had graduated first in his West Point class of 1861, "was killed along with more than two dozen of his men in the first blast of musketry that greeted his arrival."[79]

Meanwhile, the 20th Maine and the 15th Alabama were still battling it out, each gaining and loosing ground by bloody inches. "The men of these two outfits fought as if the outcome of the battle, and with it the war, depended on their valor: as indeed perhaps it did, since whoever had possession of this craggy height on the Union left would dominate the whole fishook position."[80]

Sometime during the exchange of fire, Chamberlain took a bad blow to his left thigh when a bullet was stopped by the steel scabbard of the sword hanging from his belt. He was also hit in the foot by a piece of shrapnel that entered just above the right instep. Although the inside of his boot was wet with blood and the wound caused him to limp, his concentration on the battle suppressed the pain. Through the clouds of smoke he could see his line was thinning from casualties, and could hear, beneath the roar of bullets, the undertones of wounded and dying voices. In an effort to help him, Captain Woodward of the 83rd Pennsylvania shifted some of his men to the left.   Although this provided some relief on Chamberlain's front, the waves of Rebels kept coming. Under the charges and counter-charges, Oates, too, suffered heavy losses, including a number of his officers and his own brother John. Oates writes:

> My Lieutenant-Colonel, J.B. Feagin, had lost his leg; the heroic Captain Ellison had fallen, while Captain Brainard, one of the bravest and best officers in the regiment, leading his company forward, fell, exclaiming: 'Oh God! that I could see my mother,' and instantly expired.[81]

The situation continued to worsen for Oates. The 47th Alabama on his immediate left had lost contact with the 4th Alabama, and the gap in the Rebel line allowed the 83rd Pennsylvania to begin a deadly flanking fire upon the 47th. After the 47th's commander, Lieutenant-Colonel Michael J. Bulger, was severely wounded, a number of the 47th's companies broke and retreated in confusion back up Big Round Top. This left Oates in an extremely dangerous position--both his left and right flanks were unprotected, and he was also being mysteriously fired upon at the rear of his regiment.[82]

Like his courageous adversary, Chamberlain also had problems. His right wing was out of ammunition. In less than an hour and a half, the Maine men had fired over twenty thousand bullets. In the lull following the previous charge, he was faced with two choices: retreat, or hold this ground empty-handed and watch his men be slaughtered. During this momentary break in fighting, two men on the opposite line would also have to make difficult choices. One was a Rebel sharpshooter who had Chamberlain dead in his sights on two occasions but could not pull the trigger. In a letter to Chamberlain, the man later wrote:

> You were standing in the open behind the center of your line, full exposed. I knew your rank by your uniform and your actions, and I thought it a mighty good thing to put you out of the way. I rested my gun on the rock and took steady aim. I started to pull the trigger, but some queer notion stopped me. Then I got ashamed of my weakness and went through the same motions again. I had you, perfectly certain. But that same queer something shut right down on me. I couldn't pull the trigger, and, gave it up--that is, your life.[83]

Adversaries on Little Round Top; Col. William C. Oates (left), and Col. Joshua L. Chamberlain (right).

The other Confederate grappling with a decision was Colonel Oates. Oates had lost nineteen of his of his forty-two officers, 343 of his 644 men, and, unable to obtain any reinforcements from Law, he was wrestling with the idea of retreat. Now certain that the hill before them could not be taken and that he was being surrounded on his flanks, front, and rear, Oates prepared to order a withdrawal of his troops.[84]

Chamberlain too, was preparing to give an order--a bayonet charge. Just before he sounded the command, "brave, warm-hearted Lieutenant Melcher, of the Color Company, whose Captain and nearly half of his men were down," asked if he and his company could go forward to remove the wounded men on the field. Chamberlain told him, "Yes, sir, in a moment! I am about to order a charge!"[85]

"Bayonets!" shouted Chamberlain.

The word "caught like fire, and swept along the ranks."[86] The rattle of steel followed as the shanks of metal spears clicked into rifle barrels. Later, not even Chamberlain was certain whether the order of "Forward!" was ever completed. But of one thing he was certain: determined to hold the Union's left flank "at all costs" and bent on revenge for their fallen comrades, his men did not hesitate. "With a cheer and a flash of his sword," Lieutenant H. S. Melcher was the first to spring ahead.[87] Following his brave example, the men of the 20th rushed forward with bayonets fixed and the roar of death in their guttural yells.

The charge of the 20th Maine on Little Round Top.

Although the 20th's left wing never heard Chamberlain's order, when commanding officer Ellis Spear saw the colors advancing, he signaled his men forward to prevent a break in the 20th's line. Storming helter-skelter down the rough and rocky ground, the left wing drove their opponents to a quick and scattered retreat, then unwilling or unable to stop, they intuitively swung around the base of the slope to join their advancing front. Trying to explain the stampede in tactical terms, Chamberlain wrote, "Holding fast by our right, and swinging forward with our left, we made an extended 'right wheel'."[88] "Like a great gate upon a post," was the way another witness described the swinging motion.[89]

"The rebels were confounded..."[90] Just seconds before the battle lines had been defined: now, what was left of those determined Yankees, were charging like a wild mob with raised and ready bayonets, their faces blackened with gunpowder and desperate fury. The shock caused the Rebels to break and run, and the men from Maine pursued them "like avenging demons."[91]

In that timeless realm of battle where seconds can determine defeat, it was the element of surprise that broke the Alabama Regiment--a regiment that had never been broken before. Overwhelmed by the mad rush, scores threw down their guns and surrendered on the spot; others ran, said Colonel Oates, "like a herd of wild cattle."[92] In their hasty and confused retreat, a number of Rebels ran right into the deadly fire of Captain Morrill's Company B. Morrill's marksmen, along with twelve to fifteen U.S. Sharpshooters, were concealed behind a stone wall and had been responsible for the mysterious fire that Colonel Oates had noticed earlier during the fight. When the 20th made its wild charge down Little Round Top, Company B opened fire and blasted away with a vengeance.[93]

At the same time, the rest of the regiment, caught up in the frenzied "momentum of their deed," pushed forward: killing, capturing, and continuing to drive the scattering enemy as though, said Joshua, "they thought they were on the road to Richmond."[94] During the assault, a Confederate officer fired a large revolver in Chamberlain's face. Miraculously, at pointblank range, the officer missed, allowing the tables to turn. Now, with the point of Joshua's sword at his throat, the Rebel quickly surrendered his Colt revolver with one hand, his sword with the other.[95]

Holman S. Melcher, whose courage had sparked the 20th's charge, later wrote:

> "The charging of one regiment of a brigade alone, and without orders from the brigade commander, was exceptional in the usual tactics of a battle; but it was the only way Col. Chamberlain could carry out the orders he received to "hold the position," for there would have been none remaining for that duty in a very short time had the enemy not been routed by the charge.[96]

In the wake of that final charge, the battle on the left of Little Round Top came to an end. "...I had the strongest and finest regiment in Hood's division," wrote Colonel Oates. "Its effectives numbered nearly 700 hundred officers and men. Now 225 answered at roll call, and more than one-half of my officers had been left on the field."[97] Colonel Chamberlain's estimate of Confederate casualties and captured prisoners, which was noted in his official report four days after the battle, reads as follows: "Four hundred prisoners, including two field and several line officers, were sent to the rear. These were mainly from the Fifteenth and Forty-seventh Alabama regiments, with some from the Fourth and Fifth Texas. One hundred and fifty of the enemy were found killed and wounded in our front." In the same report he also writes: "We went into the fight with 386, all told -- 358 guns. Every pioneer and musician who could carry a musket went into the ranks. Even the sick and footsore . . . took their places in line of battle..."[98]

The 20th Maine suffered 130 casualties, among these, forty men were killed or mortally wounded. This noble regiment had earned a hard-fought victory with blood and courage, and had, as the historian of the 5th Corps noted, "saved to the Union arms the historic field of Gettysburg."[99] For his "daring heroism and great tenacity in holding his position on the Little Round Top against repeated assaults, and carrying the advance position on the Great Round Top," Joshua L. Chamberlain received the Congressional Medal of Honor.[100]

In the hindsight of battle it is easy to speculate, to pinpoint mistakes, to offer theories of what could have been. But Colonel Oates was right about the crippling effect Confederate artillery would have had on the Union's line had he been allowed to hold his position on Big Round Top. Though it was through no fault of his own that his request was never heard nor acted upon, it was a lost opportunity that would continue to haunt Oates long after the war. He writes: "if General Longstreet had crowned [Big] Round Top with his artillery any time that afternoon, even though it had only been supported by the two Alabama regiments...he would have won the battle [of Gettysburg.]"[101]

Of Oates and his men, Chamberlain said: "Those brave Alabama fellows--none braver or better in either army--were victims of a surprise."[102] Of Chamberlain and his men, Oates wrote: "There never were harder fighters than the Twentieth Maine men and their gallant Colonel. His skill and persistency and the great bravery of his men saved Little Round Top and the Army of the Potomac from defeat. Great events sometimes turn on comparatively small affairs."[103]

Many times in the years to come, Joshua would revisit that rocky hill where the men from Maine earned their glory and proved their steel. He writes:

> I went--it is not long ago--to stand again upon that crest whose one day's crown of fire was passed into the blazoned cornet of fame; to look again upon the rocks whereon were laid as on the altar the lives of Vincent and O'Rorke, of Weed and Hazelett. . . . And farther on where my own young heroes mounted to fall no more--Billings, the valor of whose onward-looking eyes not death itself could quench; Kendall, almost maiden-sweet and fair, yet heeding not the bolts that dashed his life-blood on the rocks; Estes and Steele, and Noyes and Buck, lifted high above self, pure in heart as they that shall see God; and far up the rugged sides of Great Round Top, swept in darkness and silence like its own, where the impetuous Linscott halted at last before the morning star. ...I sat there alone, on the storied crest, till the sun went down as it did before

over the misty hills, and the darkness crept up the slopes, till from all earthly sight I was buried as with those before. But oh, what radiant companionship rose around, what steadfast ranks of power, what bearing of heroic souls. Oh, the glory that beamed through those nights and days. Nobody will ever know. These Gettysburg hills, which lifted up such splendid valor, and drank in such high heart's blood, shall hold the mighty secret in their bosom till the great day of revelation and recompense...[104]

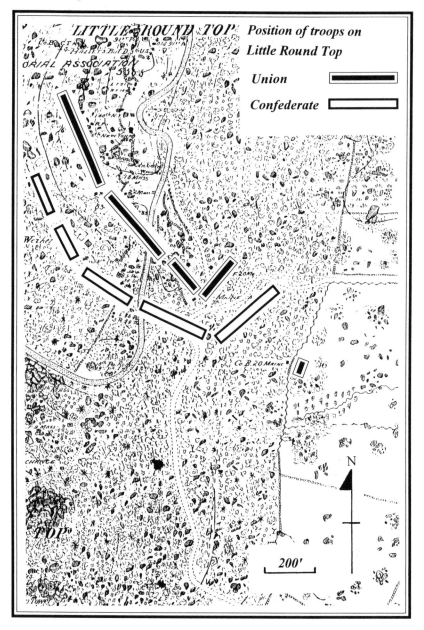

Position of troops on Little Round Top

Part Three:

So Long as Soul
Shall Answer Soul

Brigadier-General Joshua L. Chamberlain

Brigade Command

"...war is for the participants a test of character; it makes bad men worse and good men better."

-Joshua L. Chamberlain
The Passing of the Armies

Across the battlefields of Gettysburg thirteen hundred monuments stand in testament, guarding the past like silent ghosts. In search of one of those monuments, my husband and I climbed Big Round Top. The slope of this small mountain is steep, strewn with rocks, and thick with trees. Forested with maple, oak, pine, and hemlock, its underbrush is laden with hidden roots and creeping vines. Here and there, large granite boulders, formed millions of years ago, protrude from the red-tinted soil. Following the narrow dirt path, I could appreciate how difficult this climb must have been in the dark. Near the summit, through an opening in a veil of trees, we found the granite monument marking the position held by Chamberlain and his men on the night of July, 2nd, 1863.[1]

That night had been a long one for the 20th. Shortly after the Battle of Little Round Top ended, Colonel Rice (put in command of the 3rd Brigade when Vincent was mortally wounded) asked Joshua to secure a position on Big Round Top where a great number of Rebel troops had retreated. It was already dark, Chamberlain's men were exhausted from the battle, and he said he didn't have "the heart to order the poor fellows up." But it was a job that needed to be done, and after calling together the color guard, Chamberlain gathered his troops and told them of Rice's request. "I am going," said Chamberlain, "the colors will follow me. As many of my men as feel able to do so can follow us."[2]

Although they had been given a choice, not one of the soldiers stayed behind. With fixed bayonets and orders not to shoot, the 20th Maine headed toward the western woods of Big Round Top at approximately nine o'clock. Having no idea where the Confederate forces were or their numbers, Chamberlain and two hundred of his men began the risky climb up the steep and jagged mountain in the dark. Chamberlain admitted to being "nervous and apprehensive" as they quietly ascended, aware that any sound they might make could draw attention and Rebel fire. In his official report, Chamberlain writes: "We heard squads of the enemy falling back before us, and, when near the crest, we met a scattering and uncertain fire, which caused us the great loss of the gallant Lieutenant Linscott, who fell mortally wounded."[3]

It is a difficult and unnatural response for a soldier to be fired upon and not answer that fire with his own, but the 20th Maine heeded its Colonel's orders, and even captured a number of prisoners, including several officers, during its silent advance. Near the crest, the 20th posted its position two or three hundred yards above Confederate troops from Hood's division. Although they were in an isolated position, had little ammunition, and Rebels stationed so close in front of them they could hear them talking, the men from Maine remained undetected. Some of Chamberlain's pickets used the dark to their advantage. Pretending they were Texans, they were able to lure thirty-odd Rebels from the 4th Texas into capture. Throughout the night, the 20th Maine was reinforced by other regiments, and by morning, Big Round Top was in Union hands. Around ten o'clock, Joshua and his exhausted men were relieved by fresh troops. Later, the regiment was moved to the rear of the Union's left center. They were held in reserve, but never engaged in the final battle.[4]

That final battle began with the roar of 150 Confederate cannons. Their target: the center of the Union's line along Cemetery Ridge. For an hour and a half the earth shook with perhaps the most severe cannonade ever on American soil. When the smoke began to clear, 15,000 Confederate soldiers made their famous charge across the vast, open grain fields. Earlier that day, General Longstreet, who opposed a frontal attack, told Lee, "General, I have been a soldier all my life. It is my opinion that no 15,000 men ever arrayed for battle can take that position." [5]

Longstreet was right. Pickett's Charge was a blood bath. As the Confederates marched across the open fields, the "Union artillery mowed them down like blades of grass." [6] Of the 15,000 Rebels who made that daring and fatal charge, only 5,000 returned to the Confederate line. Among them was General George Pickett, whose division had suffered enormous loses. As Pickett was nearing the Confederate side, General Lee rode out to meet him. After his commander asked him to re-form his line in case of a counterattack, Pickett, still shocked from the battle and the loss of his men, replied, "General Lee, I have no division." [7]

On that third and final day of battle at Gettysburg, Lee gambled on what he believed was the weakest point in the Union's line. He lost. Shouldering the entire blame for this devastating Southern defeat, he told his men, "All this has been my fault." [8]

The war continued for two more years. During that time, General Grant would match skills with General Lee in Virginia; General William Tecumseh Sherman, who declared, "War at best is barbarism," would make his destructive March to the Sea; and Abraham Lincoln would be reelected as President.[9] Also during this time, the Union's black soldiers (recruited since early 1863, and only used for relief and manual labor) would finally be used on the battlefield. "I knew they would fight more desperately than any white troops," said one general, "...for if captured, they would be returned to slavery."[10] For these soldiers, Union victory meant freedom: for one former slave, it meant even more. Frederick Douglass, whose powerful writings in *North Star* had given voice to the concerns of his race, continuously urged free blacks to enlist. "Let the black man get upon his person the brass letters, U.S.," wrote Douglass, "and there is no power on earth which can deny that he has earned the right to citizenship."[11]

For Joshua L. Chamberlain, the last two years of the war found him on many a battlefield, where he continued to prove his ability as an officer, and to show his dignity and compassion as a human being. At General Charles Griffin's insistence, Chamberlain was given command of the 3rd Brigade in August of 1863. Griffin, along with Rice, Ames, and a number of other officers pushed for a promotion for Joshua to brigadier general, but despite their strong letters of recommendation citing his record of achievements on and off the battlefield, their requests were ignored by the political authorities in Washington. Because of his sense of modesty and his disdain for self-promotion, Chamberlain refused to write letters on his own behalf. Although Washington had ignored his recommendation, General Charles Griffin was determined that Chamberlain command the 3rd Brigade and fought against attempts to have him replaced by a full general officer. Griffin was not the only one who had faith in Chamberlain's abilities. As one of the soldiers of the 20th Maine put it, "Colonel Chamberlain had, by his uniformed kindness and courtesy, his skill and brilliant courage, endeared himself to all his men..." [12]

Despite having suffered a bout of malaria in early August of 1863, Joshua tackled his new post with enthusiasm, pushing his physical strength to the limits. Through that fall, Chamberlain and his brigade, which included his beloved 20th Maine, engaged in action along the Rappahannock River. In early November, one such encounter occurred near Rappahannock Station where the Confederates were heavily entrenched. General Griffin once said that part of what made Chamberlain an excellent officer was "his absolute indifference to danger" and that "in the field his mind worked as deliberately and quietly as it would in his own study."[13] On a day to come, that "indifference to danger" for which Chamberlain had gained a reputation would take its toll. But for this battle, which ended in Union victory, his luck held--once again, a bullet meant for the Colonel would be taken instead by his horse.[14]

After crossing Kelly's Ford a few nights later, Joshua and his men were forced to sleep in the snow. For Chamberlain, who had had a recurrent bout of malaria during the previous battle, the exposure was too much. Now suffering from both malaria and pneumonia, the unconscious Chamberlain was transported to the Officers Hospital at Georgetown Seminary on a train once used to carry cattle. When learning that her husband's condition was critical, Fanny immediately left Maine for Washington. With Fanny holding a constant vigil by his bedside, Joshua steadily improved. By December he was well enough to travel home to Maine and spent the holidays with his family. The following month, he and Fanny returned to Washington, and because Joshua was still bothered by occasional but less severe bouts of malaria, he was assigned to court-martial duty. For a man who was used to the action of the field, this job only challenged his tolerance for boredom.[15]

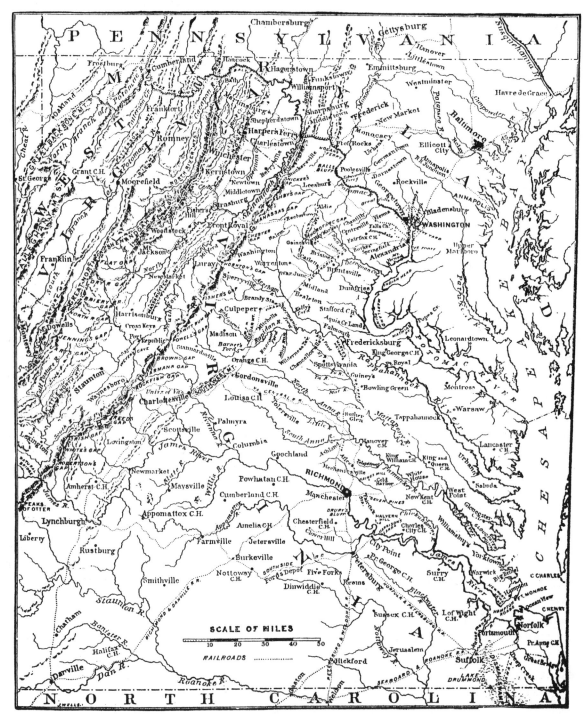

MAP OF THE VIRGINIA CAMPAIGNS.

As the first flowers of spring bloomed in Washington in 1864, the Army of the Potomac began a new campaign under a new commander--Ulysses S. Grant. President Lincoln had made Grant the General in Chief of the Union Army, but unlike his predecessor General Halleck, Grant was not about to run the war from Washington. Having given his friend Sherman full reign in the West, Grant focused his attention on the Army of Northern Virginia. Unlike those commanding the Army of the Potomac before him, Grant's objective would not be the taking of Richmond, it would be the destruction of Lee's army. The contest between the North and South's greatest generals began in a place called the Wilderness.

In the forest of the Wilderness the undergrowth was so dense that soldiers could not see beyond fifty yards in any direction. Lieutenant Holman S. Melcher of the 20th Maine said that "in that horrible thicket nearly two hundred thousand men" battled. Further describing the forest he wrote, "through it lurid fires played, and though no array of battle could be seen, there came of its depths the crackle and roll of musketry like the noisy boiling of some hell-cauldron that told the dread story of death until twenty-five thousand brave men were swallowed in its fiery vortex."[16]

When accounts of the terrible battle reached newspapers in Washington, Chamberlain became distraught. Knowing his men were engaged in battle while he was performing court martial duty was more than he could stand. Determined to return to the field where he belonged, Chamberlain managed to cut through the red tape in Washington and was back with his men within a few weeks.

General Grant "will fight us every day and every hour till the end of the war," said General Longstreet.[17] Although Grant lost 17,000 men in the Battle of the Wilderness, the new commander of the Army of the Potomac was undaunted. Instead of retreating north to rest his men, Grant pushed them south and hammered away at Lee's army during twelve days of hard fighting in Spotsylvania. During Chamberlain's absence, General Bartlett had become the commander of the 3rd Brigade, and arriving at the front just in time to see some action at Spotsylvania, Joshua eagerly resumed his old post as colonel of the 20th Maine.

The men of the 20th gave Joshua a warm welcome, but to his disappointment many familiar faces were missing among the ranks. Since Grant's campaign began, a number of the 20th's men and officers had been killed. Captain Walter Morrill, whose Company B along with some U.S. Sharpshooters had helped turn the tide for the 20th at Gettysburg, had been severely wounded in the Wilderness. Lt. Holman Melcher of Company F, who had sparked the charge at Little Round Top, had been hit in the thigh by a minie ball at Laurel Hill. Outside Joshua's regiment, others he had known and fought with had also fallen. General James C. Rice, whose last words to his aides were, "turn me with my face to the enemy," had taken his fatal bullet at Laurel Hill.[18] The bonds of friendship between Chamberlain and the men he fought with were extremely strong. The absence of his fallen comrades saddened him greatly.

One pleasure that Chamberlain did have upon returning to his regiment was being reunited with his horse Charlemagne. He had purchased the mixed Morgan the previous fall for one-hundred and fifty dollars from the government. Charlemagne had been captured from the Confederates and, having been used as a pack animal, was in poor shape when Chamberlain bought him. Joshua, who had a keen eye for horses, had seen something special in the battered and underfed animal. Under his care, the chestnut-colored horse blossomed, as did a trusting friendship between horse and rider. Charlemagne proved to be as spirited as his owner in battle, and though injured three times by shot or shell, he carried his master onto the field in almost every engagement during the rest of the war. [19]

As days turned into weeks, Grant continued to chisel away at Lee's army. Joshua and his men continued to fight, seeing action at Pole Cat Creek, North Anna River at Jericho Ford, and Bethesda Church near Cold Harbor. During the first week of June 1864, General Warren rearranged his Fifth Corps and gave Chamberlain command of a new brigade in Griffin's First Division. The 1st Brigade, nicknamed the Keystone Brigade after the state they were from, was made up of six Pennsylvania regiments, five of which were seasoned veterans. At this time, Griffin and Warren again requested that Chamberlain be promoted to brigadier general. In a letter to the War Department in Washington, Warren wrote, "Col. Chamberlain is one whose services and sufferings entitle him to the promotion and I am sure his appointment would add to my strength even more than the reinforcement of a thousand men." [20]   Despite Griffin and Warren's efforts, the War Department didn't respond, and Joshua again found himself leading a brigade at the rank and pay of colonel. For Chamberlain, accepting his new command meant having to say good-bye to the 3rd Brigade. Sadly, that meant having to say good-bye to the men of the 20th Maine as well. With these men from his home state he had shared the hell of Fredericksburg, the glory of Little Round Top, and a string of battles between and since. Years later, Chamberlain would say that "his experience with the Twentieth was the most honorable of his life." [21]

Joshua made the transition from the 3rd to the 1st Brigade with relative ease. One officer of the 1st Brigade informed his regiment that they had a "trump" of a commander in Chamberlain, and it didn't take long for the other regiments of the Keystone Brigade to come to the same conclusion. Chamberlain possessed all the qualities a soldier could hope for in a commander: intelligence, confidence, and competence. Another attribute was his ability to think under pressure, a trait he had already gained a reputation for. One evening, shortly after taking over his new post, he once again put that ability to use. He was out checking on his pickets along the Chickahominy River when suddenly he realized he had ridden too far. His first thought when he was spotted by a Rebel picket of twenty to thirty men was that he would spend the rest of the war in Libby Prison; his second thought was to focus on a means of escape.   In the dusty twilight, he knew his faded coat could pass for Confederate gray, and being close enough to discern the Rebels' uncertainty as to whether he was one of their own officers, he quickly concocted a plan whose method had proved reliable in the past. Bringing himself to his full height in the saddle, he took on the persona of a Rebel officer, snapping at the men in a southern accent, "Never mind the guard, it's after sunset!" Then, "placing his sword under his

(Above) Fifth Corps commander, Gen. G. K. Warren and staff in 1865. (Below) Gen. Charles Griffin and staff.

arm, he saluted smartly" and rode off "expecting a bullet every second before reaching the safety of some trees."[22]

   Chamberlain once said, "an officer is so absorbed by the sense of responsibility for his men, for his cause, or for the fight that the thought of personal peril has no place whatever in governing his actions."[23]   No better example of this can be given than his actions on the battlefield at Petersburg.   After Grant had tried and failed to break the Confederate line at Cold Harbor, he moved his army across the James River, bent on capturing the city of Petersburg whose railways were the bloodline for Lee's army.   Early in the battle that took place at Petersburg on the 18th of June, 1864, Chamberlain and his Keystone Brigade managed to drive back a Confederate battery that was shelling the Union's line.   The battery had been situated several hundred yards south of the Rebel's main works which were positioned on the fortified high ground of a bluff called Rives's Salient.   Rives's Salient was already naturally protected by ravines and deep railroad cuts, and to the Rebel's further advantage, its defensive line running west toward the Jerusalem Plank Road included a large earthen fort.   Fort Mahone, later renamed "Fort Damnation" by the Yankees, was situated at such an angle that its artillery could easily cover the open ground in front of Rives's Salient.   Despite these perilous conditions, Chamberlain and his men had accomplished the difficult mission of silencing the battery's artillery, forcing them and supporting infantry to retreat back to their main works.   Left out in the open, Chamberlain secured a hold on an elevated crest, and using the natural knoll for protection, he ordered his men to dig into its slope so cannon could reinforce his position.   This was the ground he was holding when, to his amazement, an officer arrived with orders for him to attack the main works in front of him.   Because he didn't recognize the officer, and knew that an attack made by his lone brigade would be asking his men to commit suicide, he risked his rank and career by sending a note to General Meade...[24]

Lines before Petersburg
June 18, 1864

   I have just received a verbal order not through the usual channels, but by a staff officer unknown to me, purporting to come from the General commanding the army, directing me to assault the main works of the enemy in my front.

   Circumstances lead me to believe the General cannot be perfectly aware of my situation, which has greatly changed within the last hour. I have just carried a crest, an advanced post occupied by the enemy's artillery, supported by infantry. I am advanced a mile beyond our own lines, and in an isolated position. On my right a deep railroad cut; my left flank in the air, with no support whatever. In my front at close range is a strongly entrenched line of infantry and artillery with projecting salients right and left, such that my advance would be swept by a cross fire, while a large fort to my left enfilades my entire advance, (as I experienced in carrying this position.) In the hollow along my front, close up to the enemy's works, appears to be bad ground, swampy, boggy, where my men would be held at a great disadvantage under a destructive fire.

I have got up three batteries and am placing them on the reverse slope of this crest, to enable me to hold against expected attack. To leave these guns behind me unsupported, their retreat cut off by the railroad cut--would expose them to loss in case of our repulse. Fully aware of the responsibility that I take, I beg to be assured that the order to attack with my single brigade is with the General's full understanding. I have here a veteran brigade of six regiments, and my responsibility for these men warrants me in wishing assurances that no mistake in communicating orders compels me to sacrifice them. From what I can see of the enemy's lines, it is my opinion that if an assault is to be made, it should be by nothing less than the whole army.

> Very respectfully,
> Joshua L. Chamberlain
> Colonel Commanding 1st Brigade,
> 1st Div. 5th Corps [25]

When the officer returned a short time later, Chamberlain's orders had been changed. The attack would be made by the whole army, but the 1st Brigade would lead the charge because of its advance position. At three o'clock in the afternoon, Joshua opened up with his artillery, then led his brigade into battle. Chamberlain writes:

> It was desperate, deadly business. The bugler sounded the "charge." Under that storm of fire the earth flew into the air, men went down like scythe-swept grain; a wall of smoke veiled the front. I had thought it necessary to lead the charge, with full staff following; but in ten minutes not a man was left mounted. My staff were scattered; my flag-bearer shot dead, my own horse down. To cheer and guide the men, where no voice could be heard, nor rank distinguished, I picked up the flag and bore it aloft, till, close upon the enemy's works, a minie-ball cut me through, and the red cross came down to the reddened, riddled earth. [26]

The minie ball made its entry just below Chamberlain's right hip, tore through his body, and lodged in his left hip socket. Despite the impact and the pain, Joshua was able to push the tip of his saber into the earth. Leaning on its hilt with both hands, he stood rigidly facing his men, ordering, "Break files to pass obstacles!" [27] Unaware that their commander was hurt, the men sped onward. With blood running down his pant leg, Chamberlain willed himself to remain standing until his men had passed. He then went down on one knee, then the other, finally collapsing to the earth already stained with his blood. When Lieutenants West Funk and Benjamin Walters saw their commander go down, they rushed to his aid and managed to carry him to slightly safer ground. Joshua was still coherent and his mind still on the battle. He ordered one of the lieutenants to tell the senior colonel to take over the brigade; the other, to get support to Bigelow's guns. Knowing it was imperative that they carry out the orders, the two lieutenants reluctantly left their commander.

"I had only strength to send two broken regiments to support the batteries, before I saw that all else was lost," said Chamberlain. "In the midst of this seething turmoil I lay half-buried by clods of up-torn earth for an hour..." upon the field he described as "air and earth cross-cut with thick-flying, hitting, plunging, burying, bursting missiles."[28] When Captain John Bigelow spotted Joshua with his field glasses, he immediately sent some men with a stretcher to retrieve him. But when the men finally reached him, Joshua, thinking he had been mortally wounded, ordered them to assist those soldiers whose injuries were less severe. Bigelow's men, however, were not about to leave the field without him. As one of them put it to Joshua, "You are not in command, sir." [29]

When Captain Tom Chamberlain learned that his brother had been critically wounded, he and two surgeons from the 3rd Brigade began searching the field hospitals, finally finding Joshua after dark. Dr. Morris Townsend of the 44th New York and Dr. Abner Shaw of the 20th Maine were both talented surgeons; the latter was also a good friend of Joshua's. By the time the surgeons arrived, Chamberlain's initial doctors had basically given up, certain that Joshua's chances of surviving were slim at best. The minie ball had caused extensive injuries; bones, soft tissue, arteries, as well as a portion of the urethra had to be repaired. Credit must be given to Dr. Townsend and Dr. Shaw for their heroic efforts and their skill. Given the primitive methods of anesthesia, surgical instrumentation, and the inability to replace blood loss, that Chamberlain even survived the lengthy operation was truly a miracle. A case history of his wound, operation, and subsequent recovery would later be recorded in The Medical and Surgical History of the War of The Rebellion.[30]

Although he had lived through the operation, the next day Joshua was in excruciating pain and was certain he was dying. In pencil, and with a shaky hand, he wrote a good-bye note to his wife...

> My darling wife I am lying mortally wounded the doctors think, but my mind & heart are at peace. Jesus Christ is my all-sufficient savior. I go to him. God bless & keep & comfort you, precious one, you have been a precious wife to me. To know & love you makes life & death beautiful. Cherish the darlings & give my love to all the dear ones. Do not grieve too much for me. We shall all soon meet. Live for the children. Give my dearest love to Father, mother & Sadie & John. Oh how happy to feel yourself forgiven. God bless you evermore precious precious one. Ever yours Lawrence [31]

General Grant, having learned of Joshua's condition, personally did what Washington had not: he promoted him to brigadier general "on the spot." In his memoirs, Grant recalls that action:

> Colonel J.L. Chamberlain, of the 20th Maine, was wounded on the 18th. He was gallantly leading his brigade at the time, as he had been in the habit of doing in all the engagements in which he had previously been engaged. He had several times been recommended for a brigadier-generalcy for gallant and meritorious conduct. On this occasion, however, I promoted

him on the spot, and forwarded a copy of my order to the War Department, asking that my act might be confirmed without any delay. This done, and at last a gallant and meritorious officer received partial justice at the hands of his government, which he had served so faithfully and so well. [32]

On June 19th, under the care of Dr. Townsend, Chamberlain was transported to City Point on the James River. Eight men took turns carrying the Colonel's stretcher and the sixteen mile hike was a taxing one for everyone involved. From City Point, Joshua was taken to the Naval Hospital in Annapolis by boat, arriving there about the same time his obituary erroneously appeared in the New York newspapers. For the first month and a half, his condition remained critical, and Fanny once again stood vigil by his bedside. By mid-August, the convulsive fever that had kept him at death's door for weeks, subsided. To everyone's surprise, especially the doctors who had treated him, Chamberlain began to improve.[33]

During the five months it took Joshua to recover, the Army of the Potomac kept Petersburg under siege, Sheridan went on a rampage through the Shenandoah Valley, and Sherman, having burned Atlanta, began his destructive March to the Sea, promising to make "Georgia howl."[34] On November 8, 1864, Lincoln was reelected, soundly beating McClellan by an electoral count of 212 to 21, and on November 18th, Chamberlain, still unable to ride a horse or walk any great distances, returned to the field. Although his spirit was willing, his body was not yet ready for the physical rigors of war, and soon after resuming his command of the 1st Brigade back in Petersburg, Joshua suffered a relapse. After undergoing further surgery in Philadelphia, he spent the remaining winter months recovering at home in Maine. The day Joshua had left Petersburg for Philadelphia, his and Fannie's fifth child had been born. Although their baby daughter, Gertrude Loraine, would not live to her first birthday, during the cold winter of 1865, her endearing presence helped to rekindle the love of a family long separated by war.[35]

Given the severity of his wound and the lengthy recuperation, most people did not expect Joshua to return to active duty. As a result of this assumption, Chamberlain was offered a number of jobs, including a position as a federal customs collector. Although these offers were tempting, Joshua felt obligated to his men and country to carry out his term of service. Explaining this sense of duty to his parents, he wrote:

> I owe the Country three years service. It is a time when every man should stand by his guns. And I am not scared or hurt enough yet to be willing to face the rear, when other men are marching to the front. It is true my incomplete recovery from my wounds would make a more quiet life desirable, & when I think of my young & dependent family the whole strength of that motive to make the most of my life comes over me. But there is no promise of life in peace, & no decree of death in war. And I am so confident of the sincerity of my motives, that I can trust my own life & the welfare of my family in the hands of Providence.[36]

By the spring of 1865, the Civil War that had torn a nation apart and shattered the lives of its people was drawing to a close. Chamberlain returned to duty just in time for the final campaign between Grant and Lee's armies, and his contribution during those final weeks of battle in Virginia was his greatest. During the fighting that took place on the Quaker Road on March 29, 1865, his ability to rally his men with courage and skill led to his brevet promotion to major general. Early in the battle, Charlemagne took off at a dead run, charging toward the enemy works way out in front of the Union's infantry. When Joshua tried to rein the horse in, it reared, and when it did, Joshua's life was once again "in the hands of Providence." Just as Charlemagne reared, a bullet passed through the horse's neck muscle, dug a furrow up the coat sleeve of Joshua's bridle arm and hit him just below the heart. Luckily, the bullet was deflected by "a leather case of field orders and a brass-mounted hand-mirror" that Chamberlain said he was carrying in his breast pocket.[37]   Ricocheting off the latter, the bullet moved around his coat, went out its back seam, struck the holstered pistol of his aide, Lieutenant Vogel, and kicked the man right out of his saddle. The force of the bullet's blow caused Chamberlain to pass out. He fell forward, his face resting against the bloodied neck of his injured animal: to those around him it appeared that the brave general had finally met his end. With great sadness, General Griffin rode up abreast of Chamberlain, and leaning out of his saddle gently placed an arm around Joshua's waist, saying, "My dear General, you are gone." Having regained consciousness in time to hear those words, Joshua lifted his head, and seeing that his line of men were breaking and retreating under the Rebel fire, said, "Yes, General I am gone." [38]

To Griffin's astonishment, Joshua kicked Charlemagne into a gallop and took off in the direction of his retreating brigade. Hatless, and his face smeared with both his and Charlemagne's blood, Joshua rode toward his men, waving his sword to rally them against retreat. Inspired by the courage of their commander, who appeared to be on his last ride into battle, the men turned and faced the enemy, eventually breaking through the Confederate line. Having forced the Rebels from their breastworks, Chamberlain started to ride back to the center of his line, and to his amazement he was greeted by both Yankee and Rebel cheers, leading him to say, "I hardly knew what world I was in."[39]

Although Charlemagne's neck injury was not severe, he needed rest and attention. Leaving him behind, Joshua set off on foot toward the front. He had only traveled a short distance when he ran into a handful of Rebels. When they demanded that he surrender, Joshua resorted to his old ploy. Hatless, his faded coat ripped, ragged, and covered with blood, he again passed himself off as a Rebel officer. In his well practiced southern accent, he said, "Surrender? What's the matter with you? What do you take me for? Don't you see these Yanks right onto us? Come along with me and let us break'em." [40]   The Rebels followed Joshua and were subsequently captured.

For Chamberlain, who had already put in an impressive day's work, the fighting was not yet over. Having located another horse to ride, he went to the assistance of his left wing which had managed to push the enemy back to the woods along the Quaker Road. Colonel Sniper, who was commanding the assault, was running into trouble. The enemy he had engaged was

Brigadier-General Joshua Lawrence Chamberlain

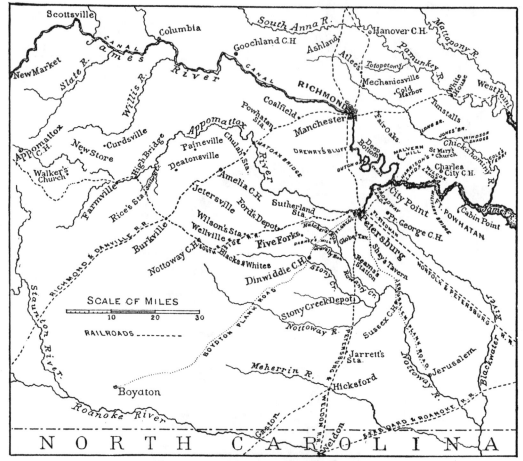

MAP OF THE PETERSBURG AND APPOMATTOX CAMPAIGNS.

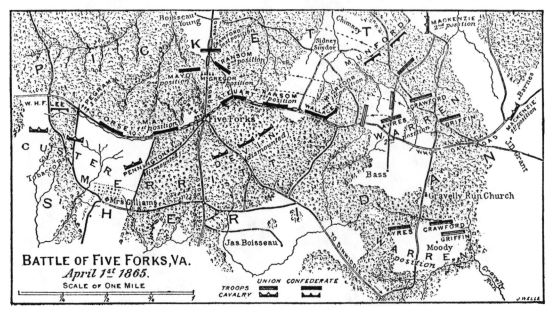

MAP OF THE BATTLE OF FIVE FORKS.

being heavily reinforced and Chamberlain easily saw that under this intense fire, his troops were loosing ground. He also saw something else. Behind him was a natural knoll--a perfect spot to place artillery. Luckily for Chamberlain, General Griffin was at the right place at the right time. General Griffin promised he would get a battery up if Chamberlain's men could hold on for another ten minutes. Charging off on his mud-spattered horse, Joshua headed for Colonel Sniper to give him the news. Three of Sniper's color-bearers had been shot, and when Chamberlain found the brave colonel, he was carrying the regimental flag forward himself.

"Once more! Try the steel! Hell for ten minutes and we are out of it!" Joshua yelled to Sniper and his men.[41]

The troops rallied, pushing the enemy back into the woods. Their fortitude during this attack provided a battery of artillery enough time to reach the field. Under Chamberlain's direction the battery placed their Napoleons along the knoll he had previously spotted. His foresight, and natural skill of using the terrain to his advantage proved vital. For the next two hours, his force of 1,700 men were able to hold off an enemy force of more than 6,000. At different intervals, both his flanks were turned and his center broken, but his troops managed to keep the enemy in check until reinforcements arrived. This remarkable feat would clear the way for the attack on the White Oak Road. General Warren, greatly impressed by Chamberlain's accomplishment, told him, "General, you have done splendid work. I am telegraphing the President. You will hear from it."[42] And he did. "For conspicuous gallantry in action on the Quaker Road, March 29, 1865," Chamberlain received the brevet commission of major-general.[43]

Two days later, in action on the White Oak Road, Joshua would unknowingly go up against troops led by General Lee himself. In a surprise attack against the Union, Lee hit Ayres' division with four brigades, causing the Union troops to retreat in panic. Once again General Warren would turn to Chamberlain, who was commanding the left flank of Griffin's division, for help. "We have come to you, " said Warren, "you know what that means." [44] Knowing they had to strike back quickly, Chamberlain refused to wait for the soldiers to repair a bridge that had been destroyed by the Rebels. Instead, he had his men wade through the waist-high stream, and after clearing the bank, pushed them forward under heavy fire for almost a mile. There, they came to an open field. On the opposite end of that field, the Rebels had established their breastworks and line of battle along the edge of the woods. At this point, Joshua received an order from Warren to halt his troops. Warren wanted to examine the area before an assault was made. But Chamberlain protested. Grant's objective was to capture the White Oak Road, and the only thing standing in the way of that goal was the waiting enemy across the field. Knowing that a delay would cost him more men in the end, Chamberlain persuaded Warren to let him proceed with the attack. Instead of using a column formation, he had his men charge across the field in loose order and with an open front, thus reducing the number of casualties from long-range rifles. Although Charlemagne had been injured just two days before, Chamberlain said, "his Morgan endurance was under him, and his Kentucky blood was up," as horse and rider led the brigade into battle, and to victory.[45] Having driven the Rebels from their entrenched position, the White Oak Road, which Grant had so desperately wanted a hold on, was now in Union hands. Of the assault that was so competently carried out, Confederate general Eppa Hunton, whose brigade had been forced to retreat during the action, said, "I thought it was one of the most gallant things I had ever seen."[46] Later, Chamberlain would confess, "Had I known of the fact that General Lee himself was personally directing affairs in our front, I might not have been so rash, or thought myself so cool."[47]

From Five Forks to Appomattox, Chamberlain continued to lead his brigade in a skillful fashion that did not go unnoticed. General Griffin stated, "it is a magnificent sight to see Chamberlain in battle"; as if to echo that comment, General Sheridan, witnessing Chamberlain in action at the battle of Five Forks, shouted on the field, "By God, that's what I like to see! General officers at the front."[48] His leadership would also be remembered by the men he led during that last campaign. One veteran stated, "The chances that came to General Chamberlain during this campaign, came to one of conceded high soldierly abilities, whose unswerving sense of honor and justice impelled him to the exercise of those abilities fully and fairly, no matter what the duty, what the danger, what the fatigue."[49]

By April 9, 1865, the Union army had converged in force at Appomattox, where Lee and his battered army had retreated. The ground upon which the presumed battle would be fought was described by Chamberlain as "a vast amphitheater, stretching a mile perhaps from crest to crest."[50] Lining its slopes and preparing to charge were 20,000 Union soldiers, backed with artillery, and in the hollow below, he said the enemy was "heading and moving in every direction, a swarming mass of chaotic confusion." Chamberlain further writes: "All this within sight of every eye on our bristling crest. Had one the heart to strike at beings so helpless, the Appomattox would become a surpassing Red Sea horror."[51] But before the fighting had hardly gotten underway, General Robert E. Lee dispatched several flags of truce at important points along his line, and Chamberlain, engaged in light fighting at the Appomattox front, was one of the recipients. A Confederate staff officer, riding alone and carrying a white towel for a flag of truce, galloped from the Rebel line straight to Chamberlain. Offering his enemy a respectful salute, the soldier told him, "Sir, I am from General Gordon. General Lee desires a cessation of hostilities until he can hear from General Grant as to the proposed surrender."[52]

And so it came to pass that on Palm Sunday of 1865, two of the greatest generals in the history of our country came together: one to offer and one to accept the surrender of the Army of Northern Virginia. The meeting took place in the parlor of Wilmer McLean's house. Chamberlain, having seen both generals en route to their destination, wrote the following:

> I felt coming in upon me a strange sense of some presence invisible but powerful--like those unearthly visitants told of in ancient story, charged with supernal message. Disquieted, I turned about, and there behind me, riding in between my two lines, appeared a commanding form, superbly mounted, richly accoutred, of imposing bearing, noble countenance, with expression

of deep sadness overmastered by deeper strength. It is no other than Robert E. Lee! . . . I sat immovable, with a certain awe and admiration. . . .Not long after, by another inleading road, appeared another form, plain, unassuming, simple, and familiar to our eyes, but to the thought as much inspiring awe as Lee in his splendor and his sadness. It is Grant! . . . Slouched hat without cord; common soldier's blouse, unbuttoned, on which, however, the four stars; high boots, mudsplashed to the top; trousers tucked inside; no sword, but the sword-hand deep in the pocket; sitting his saddle with the ease of a born master, taking no notice of anything, all his faculties gathered into intense thought and mighty calm. He seemed greater than I had ever seen him,--a look as of another world about him. No wonder I forgot altogether to salute him. Anything like that would have been too little.[53]

That night, the reality of peace finally penetrated the minds and battle-worn souls of Confederate and Union soldiers. These men who had fought each other on countless battlefields, and who had shared the blood and communion of war, now shared rations and firesides. Chamberlain would learn that night that he had been chosen by Grant to accept the formal surrender of the Confederate's infantry. That a volunteer officer was picked over West Point generals of the regular army showed the high esteem in which Chamberlain was held. To generals like Griffin, who had a strong hand in Grant's selection, it was a befitting honor. In a tribute to Chamberlain, the Keystone veterans would say, "If any one in the Fifth Army Corps maintained a spotless name and won enduring fame during the operations of that corps from the 29th of March to the 9th of April, 1865, more than commensurate with the range of the command he held, that one was Joshua L. Chamberlain."[54]

Although he was deeply touched by Grant's appointment, Chamberlain would make one request--that his old 3rd Brigade of the 1st Division, which included his beloved 20th Maine, be present. Grant wanted the ceremony to be kept simple and Joshua planned it with considerable thought. To him, this formality meant more than the surrender of arms; it meant the preservation of the Union and the surrender of slavery. "Slavery and freedom cannot live together," he once said, and "...God in his providence, in His justice, in His mercy, in His great covenant with our fathers, set slavery in the forefront" of the war.[55]

The surrender of arms at Appomattox would be a moment in history forever remembered, in part because of Chamberlain's show of compassion toward the men of the Army of Northern Virginia. On April 12, 1865, Joshua and the soldiers he had fought with formed their lines near the Appomattox Court House for the ceremony. Mounted on his faithful horse Charlemagne, Joshua watched the remains of Lee's tattered army make their way across the valley toward him. Although he deplored the cause for which the South had fought, these men about to surrender their guns and flags were soldiers whose courage he respected. He writes:

Before us in proud humiliation stood the embodiment of manhood: men whom neither toils and sufferings, nor the fact of death, or disaster, nor hopelessness could bend from their resolve; standing before us now, thin, worn, and famished, but erect, and with eyes looking level into ours, waking memories that bound us together as no other bond; --was not such manhood to be welcomed back into a Union so tested and assured?[56]

Leading the Confederate soldiers was Major General John B. Gordon, a well respected and competent commander. The humiliation Gordon felt was evident--he rode with his head slightly bowed and his gaze to the ground. All along, it had been Joshua's intention to treat the defeated soldiers with dignity. He had already informed his regimental commanders that a salute of respect would be given, and when Gordon was almost abreast of him, the Union bugle sounded. Snapping to attention, the lines of Union soldiers, regiment by regiment, shifted their rifles from "order arms" to "carry arms," the old marching salute. Moved by Chamberlain's obvious display of respect, Gordon straightened in his saddle and pivoted his horse in Joshua's direction. The touch of Gordon's spur caused his horse to rear, and as the animal lowered its head to a bow, Gordon gracefully dropped the point of his sword to the toe of his boot in salute to Chamberlain. He then commanded his own men to pass with the same position of the manual. Chamberlain described this returned salute as "honor answering honor," and "on our part not a sound of trumpet more, nor roll of drum; not a cheer, nor word nor whisper of vain-glorying, nor motion of man standing again at order, but an awed stillness rather, and breath-holding, as if it were the passing of the dead."[57]

Chamberlain's order for a salute would be criticized, but it was an order for which he said, "I sought no authority nor asked forgiveness."[58] Although harden by the realities of war, Chamberlain's sense of compassion and dignity, rooted in boyhood and nurtured by his studies at the seminary, had survived, and his respectful kindness at Appomattox would often be remembered by the people of the South. General Gordon, who after the war would become a well-known speaker, always referred to Chamberlain with utmost respect, calling him, "one of the knightliest soldiers of the Federal army."[59]

Through Grant's terms of surrender, Lee's men could return to their homes after laying down their arms and pledging their allegiance. Lincoln "wanted to see the Confederate armies disbanded and the men back at work on their farms and in the shops."[60] To the president, the Union's victory had to be treated with peace and not revenge. No Confederate commanders would be tried for treason, Confederate officers would be allowed to keep their horses and side arms. Lincoln also made it clear that the delicate diplomacy of reuniting those states that had seceded would be his sole responsibility, and he had already been at work on a reconstruction program. Unfortunately, his vision of reconstruction would never be realized. Abraham Lincoln, whose political genius and unyielding resolve had seen his country through its worst, would be cut down in his hour of glory. On Good Friday, two days after Chamberlain accepted Lee's infantry's formal surrender at Appomattox, President Lincoln was assassinated by John Wilkes Booth at Ford's Theatre in Washington D.C.[61]

Shortly after the Battle of Antietam in the fall of 1862, Lincoln had visited the Army of the Potomac at Antietam Ford. For Chamberlain, it was an experience he would never forget.

A carte-de-visite photograph of Maj.-Gen. Chamberlain, holding a pine sprig from Maine, by Alexander Gardner.

Describing Lincoln, Joshua wrote: "His figure was striking; stature and bearing uncommon and commanding."[62] On horseback, Lincoln had reviewed the troops, and as he slowly rode by, Chamberlain said:

> We could see the deep sadness in his face, and feel the burden on his heart, thinking of his great commission to save this people, and knowing that he could do this no otherwise than as he had been doing, --by and through the manliness of these men,--the valor, the steadfastness, the loyalty, the devotion, the sufferings and thousand deaths, of those into whose eyes his were looking. How he shrunk from the costly sacrifice we could see; and we took him into our hearts with answering sympathy, and gave him our pity in return.[63]

With Lincoln's death, both North and South had lost a man whose greatness was embedded in his mission to unite America in freedom--a man, in whose capable, diplomatic hands, rested the power of reconciliation. In his second inaugural address, Lincoln wrote:

> With malice toward none; with charity for all; with firmness in the right, as God gives us to see the right, let us strive on to finish the work we are in; to bind up the nation's wounds; to care for him who shall have borne the battle, and for his widow, and his orphan--to do all which may achieve and cherish a just, and a lasting peace, among ourselves, and with all nations.[64]

When Lincoln had left his hometown in 1861 to take the office of President, he told those who had gathered to bid him farewell, "I now leave, not knowing when or whether ever I may return..."[65] He would return four years later on a seven-car funeral train. The journey would cover seventeen hundred miles. Along its route, mourning Americans paid their respects, turning out by the thousands to watch the passing of a legendary president.

Encamped near Burkeville, Joshua said he and his men conducted their own memorial to Lincoln, who "had taken deep hold on the soldier's heart."[66] "The shadow of one reverenced and beloved," said Chamberlain, "was to pass before our souls that day, and we would review *him*, now."[67]   On every left arm there was tied a band of crepe; tents and sword-hilts were draped with mourning rosettes; and, "at noon," said Chamberlain, "the solemn boom of the minute-guns, speaking power and sorrow, hushed all the camp."[68]

For Chamberlain, the Civil War had brought to the forefront qualities in him that never would have been fully realized in a time of peace. Rising in rank from lieutenant colonel to brevet major general, he had "commanded troops in twenty-four battles, eight reconnaissances, and countless skirmishes," capturing "2,700 prisoners and eight battle flags."[69] For his actions at Gettysburg, he received the Congressional Medal of Honor; for his actions at Petersburg, he was promoted to brigadier general by Ulysses S. Grant; and for his actions and valor on the Quaker Road, his brevet for major general. During battle, he was wounded a total of six times. By the war's end, his courage, ability, fairness, and compassion had earned him the respect of both his comrades and his enemies. Although his army career was brief, the bonds founded with the men he fought with and the army he fought for would endure, as would the cause that had united them in battle. Chamberlain writes: "This army will live, and live on, so long as soul shall answer soul, so long as that flag watches with its stars over fields of mighty memory, so long as in its red lines a regenerated people reads the charter of its birthright, and in its field of white God's covenant with man."[70]

Major-General Joshua Lawrence Chamberlain

The Last Review of the Armies of the Union.

Part Four:
They Call for Great Men

Governor Joshua Lawrence Chamberlain

Governor

"Called to solve the problems entailed by the Civil War, his administration as Governor was marked by patience and fairness; he refused to use the power that people gave him for ends other than the people's good."[1]

-William DeWitt Hyde

In the summer of 1994, I made my first trip to Chamberlain's house in Brunswick, Maine. Joshua had moved the Federal-style cape from Potter Street to its present location at 226 Maine Street in 1867. Four years later, he raised the house, building a first floor beneath it; thus, the first floor of the old Fales house became the second floor of the new house. When completed, the Chamberlains' new home had twenty rooms, including a two-story ell, a greenhouse off the library, and a spiral oak staircase in the main hall. In the large blue and white parlor, elegantly furnished by Fannie, the Chamberlains entertained some of the most important people of their day: "Generals Grant, McClellan, Sherman, and Sheridan, literary figures like Harriet Beecher Stowe, Helen Keller, and Henry Wadsworth Longfellow, and political figures like James G. Blaine and Senator William Pitt Fessenden."[2]

The house remained in the Chamberlain family until 1939, when it was sold by Joshua's granddaughter. It was then converted into seven apartments and rented mostly to students attending Bowdoin, whose campus is situated just across the street. After years of neglect, the Chamberlain home had become so run down it seemed fated for demolition. In 1983, The Pejepscot Historical Society intervened. The restoration of Chamberlain's house has been slow and costly. At present, only a handful of the original twenty rooms have been restored and serve as a museum open to the public for guided tours.

Since my first visit, I have returned often to Chamberlain's home. I count it a privilege to wander through the rooms where he once lived, studied, wrote, and raised his family. For me it is a place where present dissolves into past, where memories of things read are vividly recalled while viewing the relics of his life: his medals, Civil War saddle, a copy of the letter he wrote to Fannie when he thought he was dying. The first time I saw his black war boots, I was reminded of how he had been injured in the foot at Gettysburg; upon closer inspection, I could see the patch over the right instep where the shrapnel had entered. With pleasure I took note of the books in his library, remembering he had never read a novel until he had gone to college, but how, before his death, his library contained over two thousand books.[3]

My favorite room is located on the second floor and is part of the original Fales house. I'm not sure why I always seem to gravitate to that room, maybe its the fireplace, or the way the light comes through its shuttered windows; whatever the reason, it is the one room where I feel at home. This was also one of the rooms Longfellow and his bride lived in while he was teaching at Bowdoin. When Longfellow returned to the college for his fiftieth class reunion, Joshua invited him to the house, and it was in this room that the great poet openly wept; it was here that "he had composed several poems while gazing into the fireplace," and here, that he admitted to having spent "the happiest years of his life." [4]

It was to the old Fales house on Potter Street that Joshua returned in the summer of 1865. He brought with him his faithful horse Charlemagne, wounds of war, and an uncertain future. For Grace and Wyllys, knowing their "Papa" was home for good must have helped to erase the loneliness and fears they had felt in his absence. Now, their father could tuck them in at night and they could fall asleep with the security of knowing he would still be there when they woke. For Fannie, it meant the hope of having a normal life again with the husband she had almost lost.

But like most returning soldiers, the adjustment back into civilian life was difficult for Chamberlain. Hampered by painful wounds that would require further surgery, and despondent over the death of his baby daughter Gertrude Loraine, who died following a brief illness shortly after his return, Chamberlain began to earnestly question his future. Accustomed to giving orders and the action of the field, the quiet life of teaching rhetoric and oratory at Bowdoin no longer satisfied him. Growing ever restless, Joshua began to search for a more challenging outlet. He discovered it in the political arena. [5]

In the aftermath of the war, Maine was struggling beneath the burden of hard economic times. Out of the state's population of six hundred thousand, 72,945 men fought for the Union during the war; the expense to the state for outfitting those troops had been costly. Of the number who served: 11,309 were wounded or discharged due to illness or disease; 8,792 died, leaving behind widows, children, and other dependents who had to deal both with the loss of loved ones and the loss of financial security. [6] The economic whiplash of the war also hit hard at some of Maine's most prosperous industries; shipbuilding was rapidly declining, and with it, the lumber trade. As a result, Maine was losing her work force of young people to better paying jobs in the industrial cities of other states and to tempting opportunities opening up in the West. On a national level, Maine also faced critical political issues that would shape the future of the country: the ratification of the 14th and 15th amendments, the impeachment of President Johnson. On a state level, it faced the heated issues of capital punishment and liquor laws.

When Gov. Samuel Cony decided not to run for office in the 1866 election, some members of the Republican party asked Joshua to consider becoming a candidate. Although wary of the consequences a political career might have on both his family life and his personal freedom,

Chamberlain was intrigued by the challenge. Feeling he was capable of doing the job, Joshua consented to have his name put on the ballot at the Republican convention.[7]

Having Chamberlain on the ticket made some party members uneasy. To them, Chamberlain was far too independent, and they wisely predicted that it would be difficult to keep him under their control once elected. Still, at the Republican convention held in Bangor in June of 1866, Chamberlain won the Republican bid for governor over Samuel E. Spring, whose supporters had "insisted not only that Chamberlain's liberalism was suspect but also that military men make poor politicians."[8] The majority of Maine people felt differently. They saw Chamberlain as a war hero and intellectual whose integrity could be trusted to help lead their state through its difficult times. That opinion was clearly reflected in the polls in September of 1866. Running for governor against Democrat Eben F. Pillsbury, Chamberlain was voted into office by "the largest majority ever polled by a gubernatorial candidate up to that time."[9]

Back then, governors served one-year terms. Chamberlain would serve four consecutive terms. During that time, he would run the state with the same dedicated skill as he had his troops on the battlefield. Following his old motto "just do it," projects he undertook as governor were not just talked about, they were carried through. Knowing that the Federal government owed the state money for subsidizing Maine troops during the war, he organized a claims commission, putting former governor Samuel Cony in charge. When the task was completed, not only had the government reimbursed the state for its Civil War claims, but those that had been carried over from the War of 1812. Chamberlain also publicized the terrible conditions at the Hospital for the Insane which had become increasingly overcrowded since the onset of the war. Pushing for the hospital's enlargement, he said, "Cells and corridors and stone walls are dreary confines for minds broken under the weight of real or fancied wrongs. . . .A brief treatment of a sane man in these crowded corridors would very soon give him a title to stay there."[10]

As might be expected, Chamberlain was an advocate for veterans and lent strong support to the orphans and widows of the Civil War. In his efforts to gain funding for the Maine Military and Naval Children's Home, he told Maine taxpayers, "Whatever means you provide for the care of these orphans, it is a duty too sacred to be slighted. The alms-house, the hovel, and the street are sad homes for the sons of martyrs."[11] He also felt the government should be responsible for providing war widows with financial support: "The widow should not be obliged to account to the Government for her husband," said Chamberlain, "but the government to the widow."[12] Throughout his terms as governor, Chamberlain would continue to bring to the public's attention his concerns in these areas. In his 1867 Governor's Address he said:

> It has been proposed to erect a monument to commemorate the virtues of the dead, which shall testify to coming generations our gratitude to heroism. But when so many widows and orphans are crying for bread, and so many wounded and over-worn are lying patiently by, hopeless of any active part in the country's rejoicings, I for one feel that our first duty is to these.[13]

Governor Joshua Lawrence Chamberlain

In the area of education, Chamberlain won the public's interest and support for the College of Agriculture and Mechanic Arts in Orono, which would later become the University of Maine. He also proposed a reform school "where the young and comparatively innocent could be separated from the incorrigible."[14] Addressing the problem of young people leaving the state for better employment, he said: "We have been too long content with the doubtful compliment that 'Maine is a good State to go from'. She must be made a good State to come to, and stay in."[15] Recognizing that it was necessary to bring industry to Maine to insure jobs and revitalize the state's economy, he searched for incentives for them to come. Believing that Maine's greatest asset and best selling point for attracting new business lay in its natural resources, especially its waterways, he ordered an in-depth survey of its major rivers. This important hydrographic survey was completed while he was still in office and would eventually help attract developers to southern Maine. Chamberlain also succeeded in encouraging Scandinavian farmers to immigrate to Maine. "Maine is surely as good a State to migrate to as Minnesota," said Joshua.[16] Hundreds of Swedish farmers settled in northern Maine due to his efforts.

These examples highlight a few of Chamberlain's accomplishments as governor. Unfortunately, these and other endeavors are largely forgotten, dimming in comparison to the stands he took on the controversial issues of his day. One such stand that gained him many enemies within his own party was his opposition to the impeachment of President Andrew Johnson. Formerly Lincoln's vice president, Johnson had taken over the office of The President after Lincoln was assassinated. Having a Congress controlled by northern Republicans made life difficult for the Democratic president from Tennessee. Congress stopped him from implementing Lincoln's post-war reconstruction plans, overrode most of his vetoes, and passed several bills to restrict presidential authority. In short, the "radical" Republicans in Washington wanted Johnson out of office and were prepared to go to any lengths to make that happen. Accusing him of various charges, including the accusation that he was involved in the plot to assassinate President Lincoln, Congress had the Judiciary Committee investigate the president with hopes of having him impeached. From February to November of 1867, a multitude of witnesses were interrogated, but the Judiciary Committee could not find a shred of evidence among the testimony to prove any of the accusations.[17]

Although their attempt had failed, the radical Republicans now had a new and better weapon to use against Johnson. One of the bills Congress had passed to limit presidential control was called the Tenure of Office Act, which stated that the president did not have the authority to fire government officials without the consent of the Senate. This act would later be declared unconstitutional by the Supreme Court. For President Johnson, the Supreme Court's ruling would be forty years too late. In 1868, Johnson was indicted by the House of Representatives on eleven charges after he defied the newly passed Office of Tenure Act and fired Secretary of War Edwin M. Stanton. Carried away with their desire to see the president ousted, Republicans attacked Johnson's character, calling him a "tyrant," "traitor," and "criminal." With the help of the press, they continued to fan the flames of impeachment until, as the Secretary of the Navy put it, "they would have voted to condemn him if some one had accused him of stepping on a dog's tail."[18] To Chamberlain, who opposed the impeachment from the start, the proceedings in Washington disgusted him. The willingness of politicians in his party to ruin the reputation and career of the president in order to attain more power for themselves, was something he could never condone. Although it was expected that he remain loyal to his party, he instead followed his conscience and sense of justice, fully realizing that his unpopular stand might ruin his own political career. Another man who had the courage to put justice before party was William Pit Fessenden, a Republican senator from Maine.

President Johnson's impeachment trial, which would come to be known as "The Great American Farce," began on March 25, 1868. The judge was Chief Justice Salmon P. Chase; the jury consisted of the Senate. During the trial, people throughout Maine held mass meetings, urging and threatening their Republican senator to find Johnson guilty. In Washington, "letters poured into" Fessenden's office, "accusing him of being at least as bad as Benedict Arnold and about as dishonorable as John Wilkes Booth."[19] In one such letter, a Mainer wrote, "Hang Johnson by the heels like a dead crow in a corn field, to frighten all his tribe."[20] But amidst the pressure and threats, Senator Fessenden continued to have the support of Governor Chamberlain. On May 26, 1868, William Pit Fessenden and six other Republican senators voted with the Democrats, finding Johnson "Not guilty." The Republicans who had worked so hard to convict the president, lost their fight by one vote. Although this would still ruin Johnson's political career, as well the careers of those Republicans who had found him innocent, they were rewarded with the satisfaction that justice had been served.[21]

Chamberlain found himself traveling down other unpopular roads as governor. While war debts to Maine cities and towns were being settled, he had received death threats after exposing discrepancies. His position on the controversial issues of liquor laws and capital punishment also gained him enemies.

At that time, Maine had a prohibition law making the manufacture, purchase, or sale, of intoxicating liquor illegal. The prohibition law was supported by other laws, one of which was the Constabulary Law. This law gave "petty officers the right to enter and search private premises on suspicion" that those living there may have liquor in their possession.[22] Although the Republican party supported this law, Chamberlain sided with the Democrats, believing it was not only an infringement on the constitutional rights of individual citizens but afforded "petty officers" a perfect opportunity to misuse their authority. Furthermore, although he felt that alcohol could drive "men to crimes which they would not otherwise commit," he believed it was not the State's job to dictate virtues and that "legislation upon what a man shall eat or drink, is certainly a pretty strong assertion of 'State rights' over those of the individual."[23] These unpopular views drew him great criticism from his party, church groups, and temperance advocates. The pressure intensified after he refused an invitation to be chairman of a temperance convention in Augusta. Because litigation on the Constabulary Law was impending, he felt it would be a conflict of interest if he attended, especially if he acted as chairman.

Chamberlain's polite refusal was "an act of official dignity and of decent courtesy to the legislature," wrote a reporter for the *Evening Post*, yet he noted that Chamberlain's ethically correct decision was used against him by "foes and false friends of the Republican party."[24] Despite the pressure, Chamberlain remained firm on his views concerning liquor laws and prohibition, and during his administration "both the Constabulary Law and that part of the liquor law requiring a jail sentence for the first offense" were repealed by the legislature.[25]

The second controversial issue that put Chamberlain on the receiving end of harsh criticism was capital punishment, which was still in place during his governorship. Personally, Chamberlain believed in it. He felt that without the threat of the death penalty criminals were more likely to commit murder. For example, at that time, a man convicted of rape received a mandatory sentence of life imprisonment (which would be the same sentence for first degree murder if capital punishment were abolished). Citing that example, Chamberlain reasoned that the criminal who commits rape, "has everything to gain and nothing to lose by adding the crime of murder."[26] Criminals found guilty of murder in the first degree were sentenced to be hanged, and, in accordance with the law, a year after the sentence was given, it was the governor's responsibility to sign the death warrant and set the date for execution. When he became governor, Joshua discovered that, with the exception of Governor Cony, his predecessors had neglected to follow through with this duty because the law put no time limit on when the governor had to issue death warrants. "Meantime," said Chamberlain, "murder goes on. Death sentences are passed, and the prison is crowded with inmates for life."[27]

Feeling it was his obligation to correct the situation, he approached the legislature on a number of occasions, asking them to either abolish capital punishment or put a time limit on when the execution had to take place. As Chamberlain put it: "if we cannot make our practice conform to our law," then "make our law agree with our practice."[28] When his repeated appeals to the legislature failed to bring results, Chamberlain, refusing to follow the path of his predecessors and ignore this unpleasant duty as governor, signed the death warrant on a rapist and murderer named Clifton Harris. This not only set off a public outcry against capital punishment but challenged the right of the State to make deals with criminals.

Although Clifton Harris had been tried, convicted, and sentenced to death for his crimes, the State's Attorney General William Frye did not protest Harris' execution until Chamberlain signed Harris' death warrant. Because Harris had "turned State's evidence," implicating an accomplice, Frye believed the sentence should be commuted to life in prison. Chamberlain disagreed. First, he felt that if the attorney general had promised or implied to Harris that his sentence would be commuted if he "turned State's evidence," then that should have been made known to the jury and judge at the time of Harris' trial. Chamberlain also had doubts about whether it was even right for the attorney general to use the promise of a lighter sentence to elicit information from one criminal for the conviction of another. As Chamberlain stated in his address:

if a person can be convicted of capital crime by evidence given under the pressure of this consummate hope of reward, then the altar of justice is no longer the asylum of innocence, and life and liberty must seek some other defense. But if this was so, let those who made the promise keep it--let them see that their witness has his reward while the case is still in their hands. But did the Attorney General avail himself of his privilege, and withdraw any portion of the indictment in token of service rendered? Did the jury in their verdict, or the judge after sentence, recommend to the mercy of the Executive? Nothing of the kind.[29]

Chamberlain also pointed out that if the attorney general promised a lighter sentence in exchange for information, it gave Harris an incentive to lie, perhaps implicating an innocent person in order to save his own life. As it was, the information that Harris provided on his supposed accomplice was not enough for the attorney general to charge the suspect, let alone build a case against him.

William Frye was not the only one to protest the execution of Harris. As a black man, Harris had suffered "the degrading influences of slavery" during childhood.[30] Citing this as the reason for his past record of violent behavior and for committing the crimes of which he had been convicted, sympathizers asked that he be shown mercy. In response to this request, Chamberlain said that the facts of Harris' life had already been considered at the time of his trial and that "they did not appear sufficient to entitle him to special grace."[31] He further stated: "It is urged that we should be merciful. But to whom? I ask. To the violator. . .or to the innocent? . . . Mercy is indeed a heavenly grace, but it should not be shown to crime. It is the crime and not the man, at which the law strikes."[32]

People against "judicial killing," said a reporter of the times, also staged protests in "the high name of humanity."[33] But Chamberlain remained firm, reminding citizens that no matter how he or the public viewed capital punishment, it was not in his power as governor to abolish it, rather it was his duty to ensure that the existing law was enforced. Clifton Harris, who had openly "boasted" about the murders he had committed, was executed by hanging. Six years after Chamberlain left office, Maine became the fourth state to abolish capital punishment.[34]

Joshua had stepped into the political ring during a difficult round, a time when the nation was still suffering the aftershocks of war, a time when strong leadership was needed most. His achievements were many, and his integrity and resolve had not been broken beneath the pressure of popular opinion or from that within his own party. But his service to Maine, both as a soldier and a statesman, did not come without cost to him or his family.

The feelings of abandonment that Fannie had experienced when her real parents gave her up as a child resurfaced when her husband went to war over her protests. Fannie again felt deserted when Joshua's desire to be governor superseded his desire to have a normal family life. Although the stress of Joshua's governorship took a toll on their marriage, trouble existed even before he decided to become a candidate. Fannie assumed that when her husband returned from war the two would resume the life they had once shared. But for Joshua and thousands of soldiers like him, things could never be what they were before the war: they were no longer the same men. The horror they had witnessed on the battlefield had forever changed them. Their memories of death and destruction, fear and courage, could never be adequately understood by anyone except those who had been there and lived through it. Thus, there was a part of Joshua that he could not share with his wife, that part where the true atrocities of war were kept. It is also likely that the war left its mark on their marriage in other ways. Accustomed to the action of battle, Joshua's restless moods must have been difficult to deal with at times, and given the severity of his wounds, the marital intimacy they had once known must have been altered to some degree.

Problems in their marriage were further compounded when Joshua became governor. Unwilling to uproot her family and move to Augusta, Fannie and Joshua were geographically separated again, and the gap created by war widened. Although Joshua traveled back and forth from Augusta to Brunswick as often as he could, his time at home was limited. It was only natural that Fannie would begin to resent his dedication to the State over that of his family. She had, after all, found herself back in the role of a single parent, having to raise the children and deal with the day to day running of the household alone. From Fannie's perspective, she had been left behind while her husband moved ahead, and, feeling depressed and rejected, she even contemplated divorce. For Joshua, who was contending with temperance groups, death threats, debates on capital punishment, and the other pressures that went with being governor, Fannie's unhappiness might have been perceived as an unwillingness to support him when he needed her encouragement most.[35]

During this turbulent period, Joshua also lost his brother John to the same disease that had taken his brother Horace. For Fannie and Joshua, the tragedy of John's death so soon after their baby's must have been emotionally trying, no doubt rekindling the anguish of having to bury their youngest daughter. Having been through so much in such a short time, it is no wonder that the Chamberlain marriage suffered beneath the burden of all these pressures. Yet Fannie and Joshua were able to overcome the difficulties that existed between them, and their mutual love and respect kept them united as man and wife for almost fifty years.

Chamberlain at 1904 Bowdoin Commencement.

College President

"The final judgment of his presidency had to await the passage of the years. With the eventual adoption of most of his reforms came the inescapable conclusion that Chamberlain was an educational prophet whose time had not yet come."

-Richard L. Sherman
Joshua Lawrence Chamberlain 1828-1914 A Sesquicentennial Tribute

One day while I was doing research on Chamberlain at Bowdoin's library, I decided to take a much needed break. Venturing outside to a nearby courtyard, I discovered that even though I had left my books behind, my subject was still with me. There in the courtyard, engraved into the smooth surface of a large sculptured stone was my favorite quote from Chamberlain's The Passing Of The Armies. This unexpected pleasure only reinforced what I had already come to know--a part of Chamberlain will always live on at Bowdoin College.

When Bowdoin President Samuel Harris decided to accept a position at Yale, Bowdoin Trustees and overseers only considered one man for his replacement. After running the state of Maine for four years, and with no plans or desire to run it for a fifth, Joshua found the offer appealing. It was a prestigious position, one that Fannie must have favored; it would not only allow Joshua more time at home with her and the children, but lighten the domestic responsibilities she had shouldered alone for so long. This opportunity would also enable Joshua to pursue his interest and new ideas in the area of education. However, having been a student and professor at Bowdoin, he was well aware that the politics of academia could be more trying than those he had encountered as an officer in the army, or even as governor. Thus, he made it clear to the trustees that he was only interested in the position if he were allowed the freedom and flexibility to make changes at the college. They agreed to his wishes and elected him president by an unanimous vote.

Chamberlain came to his new post at a time when the country was rapidly changing. It had emerged from the Civil War as a united nation; American society was moving forward, and the challenges were many. The generation that had fought and survived the bloodiest war in the history of the country was now determined that their children would have better lives and opportunities, and one way of providing that was through a good education. To meet that demand and keep abreast of the progressive steps being made by other colleges, Joshua knew that Bowdoin not only had to reform parts of its curriculum but also its attitude toward education. He believed Bowdoin had to "accept at once the challenge of the times," and initiated a number of changes to do so.[36] He established a science department and engineering course; placed an emphasis on the modern languages of French and German rather than the ancient Greek and Latin for those who elected the scientific course; and encouraged professors to treat their students as adults and to be more accessible to them both in and out of the classroom. He extended the hours of the library and did away with Saturday classes and the long winter vacation, thus allowing graduation to take place in June. Ever willing to explore new avenues of study, Chamberlain started a summer school for sciences which even allowed women to attend.[37]

Although Chamberlain had been given the leeway to make these reforms, not all of them were met without resistance. A number of the older professors felt that such changes were a threat to Bowdoin's traditional course of study which had catered to the pursuit of the ministry. Under their new president, they had seen evening prayers abolished except for Sundays, and the addition of a science department in an era when science was still looked upon with some suspicion by professors of religion. To many, Chamberlain's educational ideas were considered radical; his opinions too liberal. He believed that women had rights to higher education, saying, "Women too should have part in this high calling. Because in this sphere of things her 'rights,' her capacities, her offices, her destiny, are equal to those of man."[38] Living in a time when admitting women to the classroom was "thought to degrade a college," it is no wonder that Joshua rattled academic cages at Bowdoin.[39] Trying to share his vision of the future in a speech to students, faculty, and trustees, he said that the changing times should be "a new Elizabethan age, of dazzling discoveries, broadening science, swift-following invention, arts multiplying, civilization advancing, new fields of thought and labor..."[40] Instead of looking upon the scientific, technological, and other advancements being made by his country and by American society as being "evil" or "materialistic", he said, "...this is a good age, and we need not quarrel with it. We must understand it, if we can."[41]

In his book, Soul Of The Lion, Willard M. Wallace wrote that "Bowdoin was never the same after Chamberlain's arrival; the modern college dates from him."[42] But Chamberlain's attempts to modernize the college were not all successful. The science department, because of lack of funds and student interest, was not able to compete with the State Agricultural College in Orono, or M.I.T. in Massachusetts. After ten years it was discontinued, but during its existence it had graduated a number of great men; a dean of M.I.T.; an engineering adviser to the Chinese government; and Robert Edwin Peary, explorer of the North Pole. One program that also proved a failure was Chamberlain's military drill. As the United States was fast becoming a world power, Chamberlain believed his country's involvement in "future wars were inevitable."[43] Thus, when the federal government began encouraging colleges and universities to develop programs that would prepare and familiarize men with basic military practices and principals, Chamberlain introduced such a program at Bowdoin and recommended that Major Joseph P. Sanger be in charge of it. Sanger was well liked by the students, and for a time the military drill program was readily accepted. "Four infantry companies numbering nearly two hundred student privates, noncommissioned officers, and officers," were organized, and after the state lent the college four cannons, artillery drills were also introduced.[44] Wearing uniforms fashioned after those of West Point, the students at first took their roles seriously, but with time the novelty of drilling wore off. Resenting both the time it took away from their studies and the personal cost for their uniforms, the students finally rebelled. Pledging that they would never drill again, they signed petitions and went over Chamberlain's head, addressing the Board of Trustees directly. After negotiations failed, students were given an ultimatum: either resume their drilling or go home. The students went home. Letters from the college followed, informing parents that their sons had to return to school within ten days and agree "to comply with the laws of the college, including the requirements concerning drill, or be expelled."[45] The students returned, but the program of military drilling became optional, only to be dropped completely three years later. For Chamberlain, it was a disappointment. His experiences during the Civil War had convinced him that "our educated young men should be so instructed as to be able to assume command of men, and to direct the defense of society against its foes."[46] Of the program's failure, he admitted "perhaps it is impracticable to bring such exercises into a regular college with traditions like ours."[47] Of the rebellion, one former student would write, "Of course we were wrong, and we all went back and submitted to the rules of the College, but the backbone of the drill was broken."[48]

Although some of Chamberlain's ideas were too radical for his time, in the future some would be resurrected temporarily: for the duration of World War One, Bowdoin essentially became a military institution. And some of his ideas would become permanently institutionalized: in 1892, under President William DeWitt Hyde, Bowdoin would introduce educational departments; among these would be one for science. Chamberlain's belief that women had a right to higher education would become a reality at Bowdoin in 1971, when the college finally opened its doors to women.[49]

Outside the college, there were other events that highlighted the years during Chamberlain's presidency at Bowdoin. In 1876, Joshua was selected by Maine governor Seldon Connor to give a speech in the state's honor at the Centennial Exhibition in Philadelphia. One of the biggest events in the post-Civil War era, the Exhibition was in honor of the country's one-hundredth birthday and people from all over the country as well as the world attended. Chamberlain's speech, *Maine: Her Place in History*, was so well received by the audience and press that it was delivered again a few months later for the Maine legislature and was subsequently published as a state document. In 1878, the President of the United States, Rutherford Hayes, chose Chamberlain to be United States Commissioner of Education for the Paris Exposition. While he was there, Joshua wrote a 165 page report for the American government appraising European education with an emphasis on systems being utilized in France. The report, which was published by the United States government, was said to be at that time "the best original production on public schools abroad which has been printed in America."[50] For this effort, Chamberlain would receive a bronze medal from France.

The most harrowing event for Chamberlain occurred during Maine's great election crises. In the fall elections of 1879, none of the candidates running for governor won the majority of the popular vote. This meant it was up to the Legislature to elect the new governor. As the Republicans had just won the majority of seats in both the House and Senate, their candidate Daniel Davis was favored to win over Greenback candidate Joseph Smith, and Democratic candidate Dr. Alzono Garcelon (the current governor). Before it ever came to a vote, however, Democrats and Greenbackers began accusing Republican legislators of using "bribery and fraud" to win their newly elected positions, and their accusations became front-page news. After the current governor and his council conducted an investigation of the election returns, the power shifted. Now instead of being in the majority, the Republican legislators were in the minority, and it was their turn to cry foul play. They claimed the returns had been tampered with by Garcelon and his council and that the constitutional rights of those newly elected legislators, whose seats had been lost in the recount, had been violated. Lot M. Morrill, President Grant's Secretary of the Treasury, and former Maine governor and senator, "urged Garcelon to let the Supreme Court of the State decide on the legality of the conflicting claims."[51] The whole affair might have been resolved without incident if Republican senator James G. Blaine, had not acted rashly.

Blaine, who was determined to rescue his party, set up an armed camp of Republicans at his home next to the Capitol. Answering the show of force, Governor Garcelon positioned close to a hundred hired men in and around the Capitol, arming them with rifles and twenty-thousand rounds of ammunition, which caused the *Portland Daily Press* to dub the complex, "Fort Garcelon."[52] Meanwhile, Democrats and Greenbackers joined forces and raised their own army, setting up their headquarters in a hotel in downtown Augusta.

With a state civil war looming before them, events grew steadily out of control: Mainers descended on Augusta by the trainload, "armed to the teeth" and ready to battle for their designated parties; newspapers took sides, fueling emotions; Blaine's men skirted the lawns of his mansion with rifles aimed at Garcelon's henchmen across the way; and Augusta became "a powder keg with plenty of willing hands ready to set it off."[53] Finally, on January 5, 1880, Governor Garcelon, realizing he was in over his head, called out the State militia. As major general of the militia, it was now up to Chamberlain to "protect the public property and institutions of the State until the Governor's successor" was determined by the Supreme Court.[54] Trading college garb for uniform, Joshua took command.

Realizing that a show of military force would only intensify the already volatile situation, Joshua ordered his militia commanders to mobilize their men, but not to come to Augusta unless he gave the order. Arriving in the Capitol, Chamberlain was the only man wearing a military uniform, and "in a city swarming with riflemen" he had chosen to come unarmed.[55] Preferring to use the city police to maintain law and order, Joshua secured their support from the city's mayor, Charles E. Nash. He then convinced Governor Garcelon to disband his army of hired guns at the Capitol complex, and replaced them with regular officers from the city's police force. To insure the safekeeping of state documents, Chamberlain had them placed in the Treasury vaults and kept entrances to all executive chambers under guard.[56]

For twelve days Joshua worked out of a small office in the Capitol building, using the city's police force and the aid of its mayor to keep the "powder keg" from igniting. During this time, each of the opposing camps tried to win his favor, asking Chamberlain to recognize their candidate as Governor. Joshua refused the requests: it was a decision to be made by the Legislature, and who would comprise that body of government had to be decided by Supreme Court, not by a military commander. He also refused to be swayed by Republican pleas for loyalty to his party: his role was that of a military officer and as such, his stance must remain neutral. Because of that stance, Chamberlain soon became the focus of everyone's anger. Newspapers were quick to jump on the bandwagon, accusing him of being "The Tool of Blaine," "The Fusionist Sympathizer," "The Serpent of Brunswick," and the "Most Dangerous Man in Maine."[57] Realizing that Chamberlain could not be wooed nor bullied, his enemies decided to eliminate him, but a plot to assassinate him was spoiled when Mayor Nash caught wind of it. As a precaution, Nash "sent a squad of policemen with the General whenever he left the Capitol."[58] A scheme to kidnap him one night and keep him captive in "some remote village" while the rival camps fought it out also failed because Joshua never slept in the same place twice.[59]

In the heat of all this emotion, Chamberlain remained cool and level headed, even when facing a crowd of angry men who had come to kill him. After being warned by an aide that a gang of "twenty-five or thirty men" had gathered outside and were "bent on killing him," Chamberlain confronted the mob and gave them the chance.[60] Emerging from the building alone, Joshua descended the first two steps of the Capitol, then addressed the angry crowd:

> Men, you wish to kill me, I hear. Killing is no new thing to me. I have offered myself to be killed many times, when I no more deserved it than I do now. Some of you, I think, have been with me in those days. You understand what you want, do you? I am here to preserve the peace and honor of this State, until the rightful government is seated--whichever it may be, it is not for me to say. But it is for me to see that the laws of this State are put into effect, without fraud, without force, but with calm thought and purpose. I am here for that, and I shall do it. If anybody wants to kill me for it, here I am. Let him kill![61]

With a dramatic gesture, Joshua flung open his coat and waited. His show of bravery had caught the men off guard, and his words had made some remember his leadership, and their loyalty, on the battlefields of Gettysburg and Virginia. "By God, General," yelled one veteran,

Gen. Chamberlain with veterans belonging to the Charles A. Warren G.A.R. Post #73, Standish, Me.

as he shoved his way through the mob, "the first man that dares to lay a hand on you, I'll kill him on the spot!"[62]

Willard Wallace wrote that "although the General had resorted to melodrama, it had paid off."[63] The crowd dispersed and Joshua remained unharmed. But the crisis was not over. A plot to kill Senator Blaine was uncovered by Joshua and Mayor Nash, and after warning him of it, Blaine's views of the situation at hand began to change. Instead of using force, he now urged his party to let the Court decide the matter. But the other camp was not ready to submit to good reason. Their candidate, Joseph S. Smith, declared himself Governor and "revoked Governor Garcelon's famous Special Order Number 45" that had ordered Chamberlain to duty.[64] Joshua would not recognize Smith as the new governor however, or relinquish the duty he had been given to carry out, and when Smith dispatched a police officer to arrest him, Joshua also refused to be arrested.

Coincidentally, this would be the day that the State Supreme Court finally handed down its decision on the Legislature: the Republicans would retain the majority of seats in both the House and the Senate. The next day, Chamberlain was relieved of his duty by the State's new governor, Daniel F. Davis. To Chamberlain, Davis would write:

> In common with all the citizens of this State I have watched with great anxiety the events of the past few days, and rejoice with them in the good results of the wise and efficient measures adopted by you for the preservation of the peace and protection of the property and institutions of the State; and more especially that those results have been accomplished without resorting to military force, or permitting violence to be used.[65]

Now instead of being the "Most Dangerous Man in Maine," Chamberlain was heralded as "Champion of Civil Liberty in Maine."[66] Although he was showered with commendations and platitudes, what meant most to him were the faithful friends that had stood by him when he was considered "The Serpent of Brunswick." People like Mayor Nash; the veteran who had come forward in the crowd; the private who had fought with him at Little Round Top and had written in the height of the crises that he could raise a company of men for Chamberlain if he needed it, and that although he had lost one leg at Gettysburg, he "would be glad to risk his other leg in the defense of his old commander."[67] These and other shows of loyalty were, in themselves, a worthy reward for his service.

Returning to Bowdoin, Chamberlain continued on as its president for three more years. His decision to resign from that post in the fall of 1883 was based on a number of factors, one of them his health. He had neglected his old war wounds for too long, resulting in another operation the previous spring. He needed to recover his strength, and that meant slowing down. Joshua remained at the college for two more years, teaching political science and public law. "Between 1855 and 1885 he taught every subject in the college curriculum with the exception of Mathematics and Physical Science" and serving as an active trustee, he would remain dedicated to Bowdoin for the rest of his life.[68]

Joshua L. Chamberlain with friend.

Business and Writing

"Two of Father's companies are coming to the front, three of them in fact, and I hope he will see that he gets something for himself out of them..."

-Wyllys Chamberlain
in a letter to his mother, 1892

In the spring of 1994, my nephew, John Hamlin Deans, went on a field trip with his school to the Chamberlain Museum in Brunswick, Maine. The experience sparked a desire to know more about Joshua L. Chamberlain. Being the bright, young student that he is, John searched various bookstores and libraries for works about Chamberlain that were appropriate for his age level. Finding none, he asked if I would write one. Thus began a journey that would take me down roads I otherwise never would have traveled, each step along the way bringing new knowledge, new insight, and new friends. Although Chamberlain's acts of heroism during the war are legendary, as a writer, I found the real story laid not in the way he led his men, but in the manner in which he led his life.

After resigning as Bowdoin's president, Joshua turned his attention to the field of business. Working out of New York, Florida, and Maine, his business ventures included developing land in Florida, establishing the Ocala and Silver Springs Railroad, and holding stock and serving as president for a number of companies, including New Jersey Construction, Mutual Town and Bond of New York, and Kinetic Power.[69] Joshua's idealism and sense of duty to others were two things that motivated him. It made him an excellent officer, a trusted governor, a progressive college president, but a poor businessman. As Wyllys points out in a letter to his mother, "Father cannot ever be relied upon to look out for himself, but always for the other fellow."[70] Although Joshua's investments were many, and varied from orange groves to railroads, he would reap little financial reward, and after dealing in the world of finance for almost a decade, he gave it up, wanting "to put his strength into good clean work."[71] In regards to his father's business career, Wyllys told his mother, "our man can't be best at everything."[72]

Although Joshua's years as a businessman were not productive financially, they were productive in other ways. During this time, he became president of the Artist and Artisans Institute in New York and started a summer school for its students at his ocean home

Domhegan. In this scenic and stimulating atmosphere, up to thirty artists at a time had the privilege of studying under the Institute's founder, Professor John Ward Stimson. At a cost of only six dollars a week for room and board, Stimson's students had the opportunity to capture on canvas the beauty of Maine's coast.[73]

Another productive outlet for Chamberlain was giving speeches and lectures, for which he was in great demand. Normally reserved, in front of an audience Joshua displayed surprising theatrical talent and it was said his impromptu speeches were "when he was at his best and spoke 'winged words' that thrilled the hearts of his hearers."[74] The topics of his speeches varied with his audience, ranging from philosophy and education to the Civil War and America's future. Interwoven into his speeches were themes of loyalty, brotherhood, and spirituality, and his passion for these points of honor moved audiences whenever he spoke. His address honoring Abraham Lincoln, which was delivered in Philadelphia during a centennial celebration of the president's birthday, is considered by many to be his "masterpiece." The young Bowdoin student who had once suffered from a speech impediment had certainly come a long way.

Writing speeches and addresses paved the way for Chamberlain's greater literary contributions which included such works as, *My Story of Fredericksburg*, *Through Blood and Fire at Gettysburg*, and his book, The Passing of the Armies. His natural ability to write was enhanced by his intelligence and his need to share his experiences of the war. With honesty, emotion, and authority, he wrote in first person, capturing for his readers the incidents that effected him most. One such incident, described in the chapter "The Overture" in The Passing of The Armies, deals with the aftermath of a horrendous day of battle on the Quaker Road:

> ...I walked out alone over the field to see how it was faring for the 'unreturning brave.' It was sunset beyond the clouds; with us the murky battle-smoke and thickening mists wrapped the earth, darklier shaded in many a spot no light should look on more. Burials were even now begun; searchings, questionings, reliefs, recognitions, greetings, and farewells; last messages tenderly taken from manly lips for breaking hearts; insuppressible human moan; flickerings of heart-held song; vanishing prayer heavenward. But what could mortal do for mortal or human skill or sympathy avail for such deep need? I leaned over one and spoke to another as I passed, feeling how little now I could command. At length I kneeled above the sweet body of McEuen, where God's thought had folded its wing; and near by, where wrecks were thickly strewn, I came upon brave old Sickel lying calm and cheerful, with a shattered limb, and weakened by loss of blood while "fighting it through," but refusing to have more attention than came in his turn. Still pictured on my mind his splendid action where I had left him rallying his men, I sat down by him to give him such cheer as I could. He seemed to think I needed the comforting. The heroic flush was still on his face. "General," he whispers, smiling up, "you have the soul of the lion and the heart of the woman." "Take benediction to yourself," was the reply; "you could not have thought that, if you had not been it." And that was our thought at parting for other trial, and through after years. For so it is: might and love,--they are the all;--fatherhood and motherhood of God himself, and of every godlike man.

Still we are gathering up our wounded; first filling the bleak old Quaker meeting-house with those requiring instant attention and tenderest care, then giving our best for the many more, sheltering them as we could, or out under the brooding rain, where nature was sighing her own requiem, but even this grateful to some parched lip or throbbing wound. Still, after the descending night had wrapped the world in its softening shroud the burials were going on (for we had other things for the morrow),--strange figures on some far edge, weirdly illumined by the lurid lanterns holding their light so close, yet magnifying every form and motion of the scene, all shadow-veiled and hooded like the procession of the "misericordia." Seeking also the wounded of the enemy, led mostly by moans and supplications,--souls left so lonely, forlorn, and far away from all the caring; caring for these too, and partly for that very reason; gathering them out of the cold and rain when possible,--for "blood is thicker than water,"--we treated them as our own. "How far that little candle throws its beams!" Indeed, in the hour of sorrow and disaster do we not all belong to each other? At last, having done all possible, our much-enduring men lay down under the rain and darkness descending so close, so stifling, so benumbing, --to sleep, to dream.

For my own part, I was fain to seek a corner of the sorrow-laden Lewis house, sinking down drenched and torn in that dark, unwholesome, scarcely vital air, fitting companion of the weakest there. But first of all, drawing near a rude kitchen box, by the smouldering light of a sodden candle, steadying my nerves to compose a letter to dear, high-souled Doctor McEuen of Philadelphia, remembering his last words commending to my care his only son, with the beseeching, almost consecrating hands laid on my shoulder,--to tell him how, in the forefront of battle and in act of heroic devotion, his noble boy had been lifted to his like, and his own cherished hope merged with immortal things.

Never to be forgotten,--that night of March twenty-ninth, on the Quaker Road. All night the dismal rain swept down the darkness, deep answering deep, soaking the fields and roads, and drenching the men stretched on the ground, sore with overstrain and wounds,--living, dead, and dying all shrouded in ghastly gloom.[75]

Chamberlain gave to the battle statistics a face and name, allowing him to portray with power the horror and honor of war.   Of his book, The Passing of the Armies, one critic wrote that Chamberlain "was as great a writer as he was a fighter."[76] Joshua wrote this book in his eighties, and his memory was still as sharp as his pen. The book chronicles the Army of the Potomac's last campaign of the war, and also includes the surrender at Appomattox, the death of Lincoln, and the final review of the army during its parade in Washington. In the chapter entitled "The Last Review", Joshua describes the parade down Pennsylvania Avenue and gave his own review of both the living and the dead as the Union troops marched forward. After the 5th Corps filed by, he honored his wounded and fallen comrades with a final salute:

Have they all passed,--the Fifth Corps? Or will it ever pass? Am I left alone, or still with you all? You, of the thirteen young colonels, colleagues with me in the courts-martial and army schools of the winter camps of 1862: Vincent, of the 83rd Pennsylvania, caught up in the fiery chariot from the heights of Round Top; O'Rorke, of the 140th New York, pressing to that glorious defense, swiftly called from the head of his regiment to serener heights: Jeffords, of the 4th Michigan, thrust through by bayonets as he snatched back his lost colors from the deadly reapers of the wheat-field; Rice, of the 44th New York, crimsoning the harrowed crests at Spottsylvania with his life-blood,-- his intense soul snatched far otherwhere than his last earthly thought--"Turn my face towards the enemy!"; Welch, of the 16th Michigan, first on the ramparts at Peebles' Farm, shouting "On, boys, and over!" and receiving from on high the same order for his own daring spirit; Prescott, of the 32rd Massachusetts, who lay touching feet with me after mortal Petersburg on June 18th, under the midnight requiem of the somber pines, --I doomed of all to go, and bidding him stay,--but the weird winds were calling otherwise; Winthrop, of the 12th Regulars, before Five Forks just risen from a guest-seat at my homely luncheon on a log, within a half hour shot dead in the fore-front of the whirling charge. These gone,--and of the rest: Varney, of the 2nd Maine, worn down by prison cruelties, and returning, severely wounded in the head on the storm-swept slopes of Fredericksburg, and forced to resign the service; Hayes, of the 18th Massachusetts, cut down in the tangles of the Wilderness; Gwyn, of the 118th Pennsylvania, also sorely wounded there; Herring, of the same regiment, with a leg off at Dabney's Mill; Webb, then of the corps staff, since, highly promoted, shot in his uplifted head, fronting his brigade to the leaden storm of Spottsylvania; Locke, adjutant-general of the corps, --a bullet cutting from his very mouth the order he was giving on the flaming crests of Laurel Hill! You thirteen--seven, before the year was out--shot dead at the head of your commands; of the rest, every one desperately wounded in the thick of battle; I last of all, but here to-day,--with you, earthly or ethereal forms. "Waes Hael!"--across the rifts of vision--"Be Whole again, My Thirteen!"[77]

Gen. Joshua Lawrence Chamberlain, circa 1905.

104

Family

"My respect and affection for you & father increase the longer I live, & the more I know."

-Joshua in a letter to his mother, 1877

At Bowdoin's library, I was able to read a number of letters written by Joshua. They were originals, and aware of their value and significance, I handled them with great care. Initially, I felt uneasy reading the private thoughts he had written to others, but within some of those pages were parts of Joshua I needed to know. I believe it is through his letters that we gain our greatest insight into Joshua's feelings for his family, and as a result, we are able to see the man behind the public figure.

Throughout his life, Joshua remained close to his parents, writing and visiting the old family home in Brewer as often as he could. Just before returning from the war, he had admitted in a letter to his sister Sae, "I could not bear to lose Father or Mother any more than if I was a boy of 10."[78] In the summer of 1880, Joshua's father, who had taught him so many valuable lessons in his childhood, died at the age of seventy-nine. Eight years later, in November of 1888, Joshua would bury his mother. Every year on his birthday, Joshua had written her a letter, and his appreciation of his mother's love is clearly seen in the one she received the year before her death:

My dear Mother,

This is my birthday and I must write you my letter, as I always do to bless and thank you for my life; for all your suffering for me & tender care, and faithful guidance & good instruction. I trust I have made the life of some good to the world, and a joy to you. Perhaps I have not made all that was possible of my life, but I trust that God has still use for me, and has spared me through so many perils and so many years, for a blessing somewhere yet to be given and received. I pray that you may be kept in health and peace & that God's peace may rest in your soul. I thank Him & I thank you, for the happy little meeting we had a few days ago. I trust I can be of some comfort and use to you still in these sweet evenings of the years. Your prayers for me are always in my heart. God has answered them for my good, and will do so still. It is a day full of gratitude to you & to God for my spirit, & I am happy and ready for anything to which I may be called. May God bless & keep you.

Your loving son, Lawrence[79]

The love and guidance given to Joshua by his parents was passed along to his own children. Wyllys and Grace grew up in a household where religion and education were priorities. Despite his absences, Joshua also made sure that their home life included a healthy dose of fun. Summer days were spent at Domhegan, their large ocean home located on Middle Bay near Simpson's Point, just four miles from Brunswick. Besides riding Charlemagne, pastimes at Domhegan included swimming, fishing, and cruises along the coast to Portland and back in the family yacht. Jokingly, Joshua once said, "When I returned to Brunswick after the war I found I was a great man--so I added another story to my house."[80] In the elegant rooms of that house on Maine Street, his wife and children helped him entertain some of the most important dignitaries of their day. The excitement of having men like Henry Longfellow and Ulysses S. Grant eating at their table and sleeping in their guest rooms must have had a lasting impression on the childhood memories of Wyllys and Grace.

During his lifetime, Chamberlain would be addressed as professor, general, governor, and president. But to Grace, he was "dear old papa" and "darling boy." Joshua considered his daughter a kindred spirit; even as a child, she favored and understood his way of thinking. In his memoirs, Joshua recounts an incident that happened in church when his daughter was only two. After being "passed by" at Communion, Grace had wanted to know what Communion meant. When told "they were remembering God," she replied, "Why then do they leave me out? Don't they know that I came from God a great deal littler while ago and I can remember him a great deal better than any of these big people can. They forget me, but he does not."[81]

Her father never forgot her either, even when he was hundreds of miles away fighting for a cause his six-year-old was too young to understand. Shortly after the Battle of Chancellorsville, in a letter addressed "My dear little Daisy," he wrote, " How I should enjoy a May-walk with you and Wyllys, and what beautiful flowers we would bring home to surprise Mamma and Aunty! I often think of all our paths and sunny banks where we are always sure to find the wild flowers..."[82] While Joshua was president at Bowdoin, his "little Daisy" grew into a young woman to whom he would write: "I love you because you are a splendid soul and belong to eternity."[83] During his trip to Paris in 1878, he waltzed with his daughter at "the grand ball held in the famous Hall of Mirrors at Versailles," and just three years later, he would lead her down the aisle at the First Parish Church, where she and Horace Gwynn Allen, a Boston lawyer, exchanged vows.[84]

Like his sister, Wyllys was never far from his father's thoughts. In the interim between the Battle of Antietam and the Battle of Fredericksburg, Joshua took the time to remind Fannie in a letter that, "Wyllys wants a good big overcoat to go with his boots, & cap to keep his ears warm."[85] Whenever Joshua was home on leave from the war, life for his son "was full of happiness, games, and ponyrides."[86] Yet for Wyllys, his mother "was probably his greatest influence."[87] Given the lengthy separations between father and son during Wyllys' early childhood this is not surprising. As a young boy it must have seemed like he was always waiting for his father to come home: first from the war, then from Augusta when Joshua was governor. Having to live in his father's prominent shadow also must have been difficult, especially as Wyllys grew older. As was expected, he attended Bowdoin College, receiving his B.A. degree in 1881, and his master's degree in 1884. He then went on to study law at Boston University Law School and later practiced in both Florida and New York. Working as a lawyer in Florida, where his family owned "orange groves and other lands," his practice included, civil, equitable, and criminal law. While in Florida he said he made "very warm friendships" with the people at his church and pursued his "interest in the military," serving for several years as "lieutenant of the 'Finley Guards.'"[88] One incident he would recall about the "Finley Guards" involved having to protect "an accused from lynching by a body of mounted men." Although Wyllys was in command that night, he downplayed his role, saying with a touch of humor, "the occasion does not rank with Waterloo or Gettysburg, but we accomplished our purpose."[89]

Although he had became a lawyer, Wyllys's real love was science and inventing. After only a few years of practicing law, he gave up his career as a lawyer to undertake the vocation of inventing, focusing mostly on electrical experiments involving magnets and motors. Wyllys, who seems to have been a drifter and a dreamer, never married, and usually lived with family members while conducting his experiments. Worried about his son's ability to financially "stand on his own," Joshua wrote to him and offered some fatherly advice: "Your attention has been absorbed in the inventions in which your brain is so fertile, so that you have not got into the other stratum, or sphere, of making money of it. That is a 'worldy way' of looking at things: but it has to [be] regarded."[90] Considering Joshua's business failures, it is doubtful that Wyllys missed the irony in his father's advice.

Joshua and Fannie's love for their children, reflected the love between themselves. In a letter written to Fannie before they were married, Joshua confessed, "I *know* in *whom* all my highest hopes & dearest joys are centered I *know* in whom my whole heart can rest--so sweetly and so surely."[91] For their tenth anniversary, he gave her a bracelet which he designed himself and had specially made by Tiffany's in New York. Its intriguing design included a red enameled Maltese cross whose arms were set with eighty-four "tiny gems," and crowned with a diamond in its center. On the opposite side of the bracelet rested the blue enameled shoulder bar of a major general, each of its two stars set with a diamond. Circling the bracelet between the cross and shoulder bar were "twenty-four gold plates shaped like hourglasses," each engraved with the name of one of the twenty-four battles Joshua fought in.[92] For Joshua the Maltese cross symbolized the army he fought for; the shoulder bar with its two stars, his rank; and the hourglasses, all the hours he had spent away from his wife. Fannie treasured the bracelet, not only for its beauty and value, but for the thoughtfulness and care that had gone into its design. As Joshua had anticipated, it gave his wife great pleasure to show it off.

Fannie, who had suffered eye problems most of her life, eventually lost her sight completely. In their later years together, Joshua took to calling her "little Ma," and "many a long winter evening was made pleasant for them both when he read aloud to her."[93] For Fannie's eightieth birthday, Joshua wrote her a loving letter thanking her for her life with him.

In his note he tells her, "Your husband and children 'rise up and call you blessed'--as the old scriptures represent the crowning grace of a good woman."[94] Fannie died that fall. In reference to her blindness, it is written on her tombstone: Unveiled Oct. 18, 1905. Grief-stricken, Joshua gathered all her paintings and made a shrine of them in their home on Maine Street, and in the spring, while writing a paper on the Army of the Potomac, he included a passage in tribute to his dear wife:

> You in my soul I see, faithful watcher by my cot-side long days and nights together through the delirium of mortal anguish, -- steadfast, calm, and sweet as eternal love. We pass now quickly from each other's sight; but I know full well that where beyond these passing scenes you shall be, there will be heaven![95]

The Chamberlain family plot at Pine Grove Cemetery.

The gravestone of Joshua L. Chamberlain.

The Passing Of The Armies

"The pageant has passed. The day is over. But we linger, loath to think we shall
see them no more together--these men, these horses, these colors afield."

-Joshua L. Chamberlain
The Passing Of The Armies

Tacked up in my office, framed by an empty white wall, is a photograph of Chamberlain posing in his uniform. He stands slightly sideways, head turned away from the camera, right arm resting against the curve of a leather chair, the other held stiffly by his side, hand anchored to a hat. He looks lean, stands rigidly straight. He is thirty-six years old, and the brigadier general's star, won on the battlefield at Petersburg, rests upon his shoulder. His dark hair, with its gray threads, has a will of its own; loose strands wander independently along the high forehead, others curl helter-skelter about the ears. The long, oval face is made thinner by a crescent-shaped mustache that sweeps down from his upper lip, bordering each side of a determined and slightly cleft chin. High cheekbones and hooded brow offset a beak-like nose, the collective effect almost handsome. His eyes, self-described as gray-blue, are looking beyond the room in which he poses, as though focused on battles fought or those yet to come.

During the course of writing this book, in the pauses between ideas and words, I have looked up at his black and white photo countless times. Always I am drawn to the eyes, eager to see into them, then out of them, to know just what he is envisioning beyond that photographer's room.

Retiring from business, Joshua, who had always sought his proper post in life-- teacher, officer, governor, college president--sought yet another position of service: Collector of Customs for Portland. Portland's mayor James Baxter supported him, and in a letter to President McKinley, wrote: "For ability and high character Gen. Chamberlain stands almost without a peer."[96] But despite strong support from Baxter, senators, and others, it was not to be. Joshua, who felt he was the right man for the job, was greatly disappointed. President McKinley did, however, appoint Chamberlain Surveyor of the Port of Portland, and although it was not as challenging or prestigious a position, Joshua accepted it and carried out his duties conscientiously. The job entailed running the shipping accommodations for the Portland harbor, and Joshua soon became well recognized along Commercial Street and the waterfront. Wearing "a long, black overcoat reaching to his high-topped shoes," he could be seen strolling along the busy docks, talking with the longshoremen and other workers who had come to know and like him.[97] His hair by now was completely white, complementing his soldierly bearing, and many a time a ship officer "would inquire the identity of the distinguished-looking man on the docks, and when they learned it, they would touch their hats to him."[98]

Chamberlain's job was flexible and allowed him time to continue his writing, give speeches, and remain active in veteran organizations and numerous others he belonged to such as the National Red Cross, Bowdoin's Board of Trustees, and the Maine Institute for the Blind. Frequently, he visited his daughter in Boston. Grace and her husband Horace had three children, Eleanor, Beatrice, and Rosamond. Unable to pronounce the word General, the little girls called their grandfather "Gennie." Like most grandparents, Joshua spoiled them with love.[99]

Having suffered a relapse of ill health brought on by his chronically infected Petersburg wounds, Joshua took a leave of absence from his job to recover on the Mediterranean. During his trip, he spent most of his time in Egypt, and while staying in Cairo, developed friendships with men like "the distinguished Moslem leader, Fordure" and "the great British proconsul in Egypt, Lord Cromer."[100] "My winter on the Nile," said Chamberlain, "could not be otherwise than charming and full of historic interest."[101] Still, he was anxious for home and loved ones, and after returning to the States in the spring of 1905, he gladly resumed his Surveyorship of Portland's harbor.

In his later years, Joshua primarily lived in his house in Portland which was situated on Ocean Avenue and had a view of Back Bay. Wyllys lived with him much of the time, and though Joshua was thankful for his company, he continued to worry about Wyllys' financial future. He would also continue to work, serve, write, and give speeches. His address in Philadelphia honoring Lincoln was delivered at the age of eighty-one, and its elegance and power moved the audience to its feet in thunderous ovation.

Numerous times since the war, Joshua revisited the battleground upon which he had fought. In May of 1913, he traveled back to the rocky ground of Little Round Top a final time. He was eighty-five years old. Nearly a half a century had passed since that day when he and the men of the 20th Maine made their historic charge. Although the once young body had grown old, the mind within remained fit and unclouded. He stayed upon the stony crest beyond sunset, reflecting on that "one day's crown of fire" that had "passed into the blazoned coronet of fame."[102] With clarity, he remembered his fallen comrades, the "unforgotten sons of God," and felt about him "their radiant companionship" as he "sat there alone, on the storied crest."[103]

Nine months later, with Grace and Wyllys by his side, Joshua Chamberlain died. On February 27, 1914, three days after his death, funeral services took place both in Portland and Brunswick. Businesses closed, flags flew at half mast, and the people of Maine turned out by the thousands. Some came to honor the war hero, others, the college president; some paid tribute to his service to his State, others, to his fellow man.   Portland's City Hall was full beyond capacity; Beethoven's funeral march "Upon the Death of a Hero" drifted into the snow-covered streets where thousands more waited, remembering the man who was "always reaching for his checkbook to help a sick or disabled veteran or war widow."[104]

Upon his flag-draped casket rested his sword, both were put aboard the train at Union Station and carried home to Brunswick.   There, funeral services were conducted at the First Parish Church whose history was part of his own: this was where he had given that first embarrassing speech, where he redeemed himself three years later, and many times after; this is where he exchanged vows with Fannie, where together they had said their spiritual farewells to their infants; down its center aisle he had walked his daughter to the alter and marriage; behind its pulpit rose the stained glass window he designed and donated in memory of his father-in-law, Reverend George E. Adams, who had ministered the congregation for over forty years.   This was where he held the funeral for his beloved wife.   He had asked that the same be done for him.

A memorial written by the Military Order of the Loyal Legion included a passage from General Morris Schaaf's book Sunset of the Confederacy.   Schaaf begins by telling why he thinks Chamberlain was selected to accept the Confederate surrender at Appomattox:

> I believe that the selection of Chamberlain to represent the Army of the Potomac was providential in this, that he, in the way he discharged his duty, represented the spiritually-real of the world. And by this I mean the lofty conceptions of what in human conduct is manly and merciful, showing in daily life consideration for others and on the battlefield linking courage with magnanimity and sharing an honorable enemy's woes. . .[105]

After describing Chamberlain's salute to Gordon, Schaaf writes:

> Great in the broad and high sense, was the cause battled for and spontaneous and knightly was this act of Chamberlain's, lending a permanent glow to the close of the war like that of banded evening clouds at the end of an all-day beating rain.   It came from the heart and it went to the heart; and when 'taps' shall sound for Chamberlain I wish that I could be in hearing, hear Maine's granite coast with its green islands and moon-light reflecting coves taking them up in succession from Portland to Eastport, and as the ocean's voice dies away, hear her vast wilderness of hemlock, spruce and pine repeating them with majestic pride for her beloved son.[106]

On that February day in 1914, Joshua Chamberlain was laid to rest in Pine Grove Cemetery, bordering the campus of the college he served and cherished.   The National Guard discharged their rifles in salute, then bidding a final goodnight, "Taps" followed.   It was a cold and clear day.   The sounds carried through the Bowdoin pines and far into the distance.

Photo Credits

Page II: Bedford Hayes Collection; Page 1: Bedford Hayes Collection; 2: Pejepscot Historical Society; 5: Pejepscot Historical Society; 9: Bedford Hayes Collection; 14: Bedford Hayes Collection; 17: Pejepscot Historical Society; 18: Pejepscot Historical Society; 21: Pejepscot Historical Society; 22: Maine State Archives; 25: William B. Styple; 28: Bedford Hayes; 34: MASS/MOLLUS, United States Army Military History Institute (USAMHI); 45: Photos by Author; 48: (top)Maine Historical Preservation Committee, (bottom) Maine Historical Society; 50: (left) USAMHI, (right) James C. Frasca Collection; 54: Deeds of Valor; 55: Library of Congress; 56: USAMHI; 63: (top) Christine Wisan, (bottom)USAMHI; 68: Bedford Hayes Collection; 75: Bedford Hayes Collection; 77: Maine State Archives; 78: Library of Congress; 79: Pejepscot Historical Society; 96: Bedford Hayes Collection; 98: Library of Congress; 103: Library of Congress; 107: Photo by Author;108: Photo by Author.

Instructions For Reading Notes

* Source of general information is listed as : See, author's name, title of book. For example--See Wallace, <u>Soul Of The Lion</u>.

* In cases of direct quotes, it is listed as: author's name, title of book, page number from which the quote was taken. For example--Wallace, <u>Soul Of The Lion</u>, 32.

* The first time a book is used in the notes, information will include where it was published, name of publisher, date of publication. Example--See Willard M. Wallace, <u>Soul Of The Lion</u> (Gettysburg, Pennsylvania: Stan Clark Military Books, 1960)

* When the source of information is the same as the number right before it, Ibid., is used. For example--45 See Wallace, <u>Soul Of The Lion</u>.

    46 <u>Ibid</u>.

<u>Ibid</u>., here means that the source for number 46 is the same as 45. If in some cases the source is the same, but a direct quote is used, then the page number of the quote is added. Example--46 <u>Ibid</u>., 32.

* Quotes and general information drawn from Chamberlain's *Early Memoirs* were used from the magazine "Bowdoin," Spring/Summer, 1991, as this source is more readily available to readers. The original is kept in the Bowdoin Library and is very old and delicate. As only a portion of the manuscript exists, authorities are not certain if Chamberlain completed the work, or if it was just lost.

* Also included in the notes are certain terms and additional information I felt readers might be interested in. These are marked by a *

Notes On Part One

1 See Alice Rains Trulock, <u>In the Hands of Providence</u> (Chapel Hill and London: The University of North Carolina Press, 1992); See Willard M. Wallace, <u>Soul Of The Lion</u> (Gettysburg, Pennsylvania: Stan Clark Military Books, 1960).

2 See The <u>Volume Library 2</u> (Nashville, Tennessee: The Southwestern Company, 1989), under United States History; See Gorham Munson, Penobscot Down East Paradise (Philadelphia and New York: J.B. Lippincott Company, 1959).

3 See Trulock, <u>In the Hands of Providence</u>; See Gorham Munson, Penobscot Down East Paradise.

4 Chamberlain, *Early Memoirs* ("Bowdoin," Spring/Summer, Vol. 64, No.1, 1991) 4; See Richard L. Sherman, <u>Joshua Lawrence Chamberlain 1828-1914 A Sesquicentennial Tribute</u> (Brunswick, Me.: Brunswick Publishing Company, 1978)

5 Chamberlain, *Early Memoirs*, 3. (dialog directly quoted, asides by author)

6 See Trulock, In the Hands of Providence; See Wallace, Soul Of The Lion; See John J. Pullen, The Twentieth Maine A Volunteer Regiment In The Civil War, Dayton, Ohio; Morningside House, Inc., 1991)

7 See Wallace, Soul Of The Lion; See Trulock, In the Hands of Providence.

* The Penobscots--Tribe of Algonquin-speaking Native Americans living in Maine. The word means, "where the rocks widen or open (spread) out." "Today Penobscot land consists of a reservation in Maine and territory acquired since the Maine Indian Settlement Act of 1980. The reservation itself consists of about 200 islands in the Penobscot River between Old Town and Medway--about 4800 acres. There is only one major settlement, on Indian Island, with nearly 600 people." [Maine Indian Program of the New England Regional Office of the American Friends Service Committee, The Wabanakis of Maine and the Maritimes (Bath, Maine: Maine Indian Program, 1989) D-11 & D-12.

8 See Munson, Penobscot Down East Paradise; See Wallace, Soul Of The Lion;   See Trulock, In the Hands of Providence.

* War of 1812--a war between Great Britain and the United States; started over Britain's interference with American shipping. At the time the war was fought, the British were also at war with France, which was to America's advantage. In the beginning of the war, the United States lost many battles; the British even managed to capture Washington D.C. The greatest victory for the Americans during this conflict happened in the south, when General Andrew Jackson led troops against the enemy at the mouth of the Mississippi River, and drove the British out of New Orleans. A peace treaty between the two countries was signed in Belgium in December 1814. This treaty was known as the Treaty of Ghent.

* During the war of 1812, Chamberlain's grandfather would suffer a great financial loss when his shipbuilding business was destroyed. In 1817, he moved six miles upriver to Brewer where he bought a farm.

9 Chamberlain, *Early Memoirs*, 5, & 6.

10 See Trulock, In the Hands of Providence; See Wallace, Soul Of The Lion.

* French and Indian Wars--(1689-1763) Four consecutive wars fought between the British and the French over territory and commerce in North America. The last of these wars, referred to as the Seven Years' War, began over land claims concerning the Ohio River Valley. Both sides were supported by Indian allies: the Hurons with the French; the Iroquois with the British. George Washington, who was only twenty-one at the time, commanded the Virginia militia in the attack against the French which touched off this final war. The Seven Years War ended with a British victory in 1763.

* Revolutionary War--war in which the colonies in North America won their independence from Great Britain. On July, 4, 1776, The Declaration Of Independence was adopted by the Continental Congress. The war began in 1775 and ended in 1783. This time George Washington would be commander-in-chief of the American army.

* Aroostook War--began over a boundary dispute between Maine and New Brunswick Canada concerning the St. Lawrence and St. John rivers. At stake were valuable timberlands. A "bloodless war" (no one was killed), the U.S.-Canada boundary was settled diplomatically with the Ashburton Treaty in 1842.

  * Languages that Joshua learned: German, French, Latin, Greek, Hebrew, Syriac, Arabic, Italian, Spanish, Norse, and Old English.

11 Chamberlain, *Early Memoirs*, 3.

12 *Whipped For Chewing Tobacco: Gen. Chamberlain Got the Best of Capt. Arey: Only His Authority as Teacher Allowed Him to Do It*: undated; newspaper's name unlisted; Chamberlain files, Pejepscot Historical Society.

13 Trulock, In the Hands of Providence, 36.

* In her book, Trulock explained that a singing school was more of a social event; the term "court" meant to date.

14 See Chamberlain, *Early Memoirs*; See Wallace, Soul Of The Lion.

15 Chamberlain, *Early Memoirs*, 5.

* That Chamberlain was allowed to join the Freshmen class as it began its second semester was most unusual. The exam he passed that allowed him to do so, and which he says was arranged as a special favor, was most likely organized at the request of his Latin tutor William Hyde, who had graduated from Bowdoin in 1842.

16 Ibid., 5; See Nehemiah Cleaveland, History of Bowdoin College with Biographical Sketches of its Graduates (Boston: James Ripley Osgood & Company, 1882).

17 Chamberlain, *Early Memoirs*, 6.

18 Ibid., 8.

19 Ibid., 8.

20 Ibid., 8 & 9.

21 "Millitary Order of The Loyal Legion of The United States," Tribute to the Memory of Joshua Chamberlain, 12.

22 Chamberlain, *Early Memoirs*,9.

23 Ibid., 9; See Trulock, In the Hands of Providence.

24 Ibid., 9.

25 See Ibid.; See Wallace, The Soul Of The Lion.

26 Chamberlain, *Early Memoirs*, 10.

27 Ibid., 10.

28 Ibid., 10.

29 Ibid., 10.

* Synopsis of Uncle Tom's Cabin --When Mr. Shelby, who owns a plantation in the south, finds himself in debt, he is forced to sell two of his slaves. One is Tom, a gentle black man with a remarkable faith in God. The other is the four-year-old son of a slave named Eliza.

When Eliza discovers her son is to be sold away from her, she and son escape during the night. With the help of the Underground Railroad, she and her husband George are reunited. Together with their son, they begin the dangerous journey north to Canada and freedom. Meanwhile, Tom is forced to leave his wife and children and is sold down river to a kind man named St. Clare, whose little daughter, Eva, forms a special bond with Tom. Through a twist of fate, Tom is sold again. His new overseer, Simon Legree, is heartless and evil, and it is under his cruel hand that gentle Tom will meet his death and his maker.

Uncle Tom's Cabin, is rich with characters that movingly tell a story that needed to be heard. Through the eyes of both slave and owner, the author exposed slavery for what it was, and why it shouldn't be. Powerfully written, it chipped away at the heart and soul of its readers, and challenged their humanity, and sense of justice.

* Harriet Beecher Stowe (1811-1896)--A remarkable writer and woman, Stowe, like Chamberlain was deeply religious. While her father was president of Lane Theological Seminary in Cincinnati, Harriet witness the hardships of slavery in those communities across the Ohio River. She also used to visit the home of a schoolmate who lived in the slave state of Kentucky, which gave her a close look at the southern way of life. In 1836, she married Professor Calvin Stowe, and would eventually become the mother of six children.

Harriet Beecher Stowe detested slavery. In 1837, she and her husband helped a fugitive slave escape through the Underground Railroad. After the Fugitive Slave Act was passed in 1850, which allowed slaves to be hunted down in free states, she decided to write, Uncle Tom's Cabin; her inspiration for the book, she said, came to her while attending Sunday service at the First Parish Church in Brunswick, Maine. By 1860, her book had been reprinted in twenty-two languages, and was only second to the Bible in popularity. Stowe would continue to write throughout her life. Among her works are The Minister's Wooing, and Oldtown Folks. In 1910, Harriet Beecher Stowe was elected to the Hall of Fame.

*Hall of Fame: established in 1900, the Hall of Fame is a shrine on New York University campus that honors distinguished Americans with memorial busts and tablets. Every five years, a committee selects additions from persons dead more than twenty-five years. Other American writers who have been elected to the Hall of Fame include: Samuel Clemens (Mark Twain), Nathaniel Hawthorne, Henry Wadswoth Longfellow, and Henry David Thoreau.

30 Chamberlain, *Early Memoirs*, 10.

31 See Trulock, In the Hands of Providence; See Wallace, Soul Of The Lion.

* In her notes, Trulock says that Fannie was about five when she went to live with Reverend Adams and his wife in Brunswick. According to Julia Colvin Oehmig, Curator of the Pejepscot Historical Society, new research has shown Fannie was closer to four.

* Amelia Adams (Fannie's natural mother) was Ashur Adams' third wife. Fannie's siblings in Boston included brothers, Samuel and George Wyllys, sisters Charlotte, and Mary, and half-sister Katherine. At the time of Fannie's departure to Brunswick, George Wyllys would have been fourteen, and sister Charlotte, twelve. Although Fannie came to consider Reverend

Adams and his wife as her parents, she still kept in contact with her family in Boston. Often in her letters to Joshua she referred to her natural parents as her "Boston parents", and to Reverend Adams and his wife as her "Brunswick parents."

* Reverend Adams and his wife later adopted Anna D. Davis, the granddaughter of a member of the Bowdoin medical faculty.

32 Chamberlain, *Early Memoirs*, 10.

33 Letter from Fannie Adams (Milledgeville) to Lawrence Chamberlain, June, 23, 1853. (Chamberlain files, Pejepscot Historical Society)

* Joshua and Fannie's letters to each other were at times very romantic. In a letter to Fannie dated 6/7/52, Joshua writes: "May the shunshine but give growth & beauty to the twining tendrils of our hearts, & the storms only strengthen them & bind us closer."

34 Trulock, In the Hands of Providence, 52.

35 See Chamberlain, *Early Memoirs*; See Trulock, In the Hands of Providence.

36 Trulock, In the Hands of Providence, 8.

37 See Ibid.; See Harriet Beecher Stowe, Stowe, Three Novels: Uncle Tom's Cabin , The Minister's Wooing, Oldtown Folks (New York, N.Y.: The Library of America, 1982)

* Although the Civil War would begin over union and state's rights, when President Lincoln met author Harriet Beecher Stowe in 1861, he called her, "the little woman who wrote the book that made this great war." [Ibid., inside cover].

38 Chamberlain, *Early Memoirs*, 11; See Trulock, In the Hands of Providence.

* Joshua and Fannie were married by Fannie's father, Reverend George E. Adams, who was the minister of the First Parish Church. When Joshua and Fannie first started dating, Reverend Adams was skeptical about the young man from Brewer. After all, he had seen too many of the Bowdoin boys date local girls only to leave them behind when their college years were over. Not wanting the same thing to happen to his daughter, he at first discouraged her relationship with Chamberlain. With time, however, his concerns were put to rest, and between him and Joshua there would grow a deep affection. The stained glass window behind the altar at the First Parish Church was donated by Chamberlain in memory of his beloved father-in-law.

39 See Bruce Catton, The American Heritage Picture History of THE CIVIL WAR (New York-Toronto-London-Sydney-Auckland: Random House, 1980) ; See Government/Law, The Volume Library 1.

* The Fugitive Slave Act stated that it was illegal for slaves to escape to free states; that any citizens caught helping them do so would be subjected to criminal charges, and that slave owners had the legal right to recapture and return by force any of their former slaves that were now living in free states. This Act had the exact opposite result of what was intended. Instead of peacefully standing by and letting slave owners kidnap their former slaves, sympathetic northerners increased their aide to the fugitives, many offering their homes as "safe houses." The activity of the Underground Railroad grew significantly, enabling thousands of slaves to follow the "North Star" to Canada safely. Harriet Tubman, a black woman and former slave on a Maryland plantation, would make nineteen daring trips to the south and with the efforts of the Underground Railroad, would bring over three hundred slaves to freedom. During the Civil War, this remarkably brave woman would also act as a guide and spy for the Union Army.

* Dred Scott was a black slave who sued his owner for freedom on the grounds that his master, an army surgeon, had taken him to live in the free states of Illinois and Wisconsin. Scott argued that this circumstance automatically made him a free man. The Supreme Court's landmark decision in the case was nullified by the 13th and 14th amendments.

40 Trulock, In the Hands of Providence, 56.

41 See Ibid.; See *United States History*, The Volume Library 2.

42 Chamberlain *Early Memoirs*, 11.

43 See *United States History*, The Volume Library 2.

44 Swafford Johnson, Great Battles of The Civil War Northern Victories (New York: Crescent Books, 1991) 9.

45 Trulock, In the Hands of Providence, 60 & 61; See United States History, The Volume Library 2.

* Alice Rains Trulock was the biographer who humorously wrote about the Bowdoin students marching down Maine Street.

46 Letter from Joshua Chamberlain to his sister Sae; February, 4, 1862; Chamberlain's collection of letters at Bowdoin College.

47 See Chamberlain, *Early Memoirs*; See Wallace, Soul Of The Lion; See Trulock, In the Hands of Providence.

* Because of his promotion to Professor of Modern Languages, Chamberlain was entitled to a two-year leave of absence to study and travel in Europe, expenses and salary paid by the college. Joshua would use this avenue as a way to enlist--he would take the leave of absence, but instead of going to Europe, he would go to war. None of Joshua's fellow professors wanted him to enlist, partly because they liked him, but mostly because they feared that if something were to happen to him, his vacant position might be filled by someone whose views differed from their own.   When their attempts to discourage him failed, they sent a representative to Governor Washburn informing the governor that Professor Chamberlain was "no fighter, but only a mild-mannered commonplace student," and therefore would make a terrible officer. As Joshua put it, "It was indeed a strange exhibition of affection." [Chamberlain, *Early Memoirs*, 12]

 * Joshua and his father rarely agreed when it came to politics, and the Civil War was a perfect example. Although his father objected to slavery, he felt that if the south wanted to leave the Union in order to retain it, they had the right to do so. This did not mean he was in agreement with the Union being divided, it meant he felt under the circumstances, it would be better to have two countries than to subject the lives of so many to a blood bath of war. [See Sam E. Conner, *Chamberlains, Maine History Fame, Were Opposed in Politics* (Lewiston Journal, Oct. 3, 1942)

* Joshua's father would tell him, "tis not our war," but knowing his son couldn't be convinced that it wasn't, he also said, "Come home with honor, as I know you will..." [Trulock, In the Hands of Providence, 25]

* Tom Chamberlain would enlist right after his older brother, and the two would enter the war with the same regiment.

Notes On Part Two

Reader Information:

Joshua Chamberlain wrote numerous articles about his war experiences which were published in different magazines and newspapers during his lifetime. One of these articles, Through Blood & Fire at Gettysburg, was later republished in 1994 by Stan Clark Military Books. The latter article as well as a number of others where also compiled into a book published by Stan Clark Military Books, entitled "Bayonet! Forward" My Civil War Reminiscences. As these two sources are readily available to readers, I have used them for references and quotes. The original source of publication for these works included in His Proper Post, will be listed here:

● General Joshua L. Chamberlain, "My Story of Fredericksburg" (New York: *Cosmopolitan Magazine*, December 1912).

● General Joshua L. Chamberlain, "Through Blood and Fire at Gettysburg" (New York: *Hearst's Magazine*, June 1913).

● General Joshua L. Chamberlain, "Reminiscences of Petersburg and Appomattox" (Bangor, Maine: *Bangor Daily Commercial*, March 3, 1904)

* Chamberlain's book The Passing of the Armies, was originally published the year after his death by G.H. Putnam, (New York, 1915) and was republished by Stan Clark Military Books in 1994.

1 General Joshua Lawrence Chamberlain, Through Blood & Fire At Gettysburg (Gettysburg, Pennsylvania: Stan Clark Military Books, 1994) 10.

2 Bruce Catton, The American Heritage Picture History of THE CIVIL WAR (New York/Avenel, New Jersey: American Heritage/ Wings Books, 1988) 329.

3 See Ibid. (under *Wheat Field and Peach Orchard*, and *Crisis on the Union Right*,)

4 Trulock, In the Hands of Providence, 21-22.

* Trulock lists the number of men of the 20th Maine as 979; Pullen wrote "just under a thousand."

5 Pullen, The Twentieth Maine, 2.

* As Maine was suffering an economic slump prior to the war, a number of men enlisted just for the money: pay for a private was thirteen dollars a month.

* Chamberlain and the men of the 20th enlisted as volunteers. The draft would not be initiated until March of 1863. Although the draft would call for all able-bodied men between ages 20-45, men who could pay three-hundred dollars or find a substitute to take their place were exempt.

6 See The Volume Library 2 (under *The Civil War*, and *Biographies of Famous Men and Woman*); See Catton, THE CIVIL WAR; See Swafford Johnson, Great Battles of THE CIVIL WAR Northern Victories (New York; Cresent Books, 1991).

* Confederates usually named battles after the towns they were in or near; Union troops named them after rivers, or streams--for example, the Battle of Bull Run, so called by the Yankees, was the Battle of Manassas to the Rebels.

7 Pullen, The Twentieth Maine, 18; See Trulock, In the Hands of Providence.

8 Trulock, In the Hands of Providence, 25.

9 Ibid., 65.

* Because they were difficult to clean and take care of, soldiers of the 20th exchanged Enfield rifles for Springfields whenever they could. Chamberlain makes mention of this in his official report written four days after the Little Round Top Battle. According to him, the Enfield rifles "did not stand service well."

10 See Pullen, The Twentieth Maine; See Trulock, In the Hands of Providence.

11 Robert Hunt Rhodes, All For The Union, The Civil War Diary and Letters of Elisha Hunt Rhodes (New York: Orion Books 1985), 85. *quote was from Rhodes.

12 William B. Styple, With A Flash Of His Sword; The Writings of Major Holman S. Melcher 20th Maine Infantry (Kearny, N.J.: Belle Grove Publishing Co., 1994), 5; See Trulock, In the Hands of Providence; See Wallace, The Soul Of The Lion.

13 Trulock, In the Hands of Providence, 68-69

14 See Catton, THE CIVIL WAR; See Pullen, The Twentieth Maine; See Trulock, In the Hands of Providence.

15 Wallace, Soul Of The Lion, 42; See Pullen, The Twentieth Maine; See Trulock, In the Hands of Providence.

16 Trulock, In the Hands of Providence, 8.

17 Ibid., 77.

18 Ibid., 83.

19 Ibid., 79.

20 See Catton, THE CIVIL WAR; See Trulock, In the Hands of Providence; See Wallace, The Soul Of The Lion.

* Catton states that the estimated death rate due to disease versus combat loss was 2½ to 1 for the Union; 3 to 1 for the Confederates.

* During the Civil War doctors were medically unaware of what caused infections or diseases. Sterilization of instruments was nonexistent, as a result, infections were spread from one patient to the next by way of contaminated instruments and supplies. Confederate surgeons did discover a decrease in infected wounds after they began boiling horse hair to make it pliable for suture material (horse hair was substituted for silk because they were unable to attain it) By boiling, they had unknowingly eliminated bacteria from their suture material, thus reducing the rate of infection. Doctors also discovered that the use of maggots helped eliminate gangrenous tissue.

* The spread of measles, small pox, and other diseases was rampant among both armies, and soldiers who hailed from isolated farms and rural areas were more susceptible, because many had never been exposed to these diseases and had no immunity against them.

21 See Catton, THE CIVIL WAR; See Trulock, In the Hands of Providence; See Pullen, The Twentieth Maine.

* Under Burnside the Army of the Potomac was divided into three Grand Divisions consisting of two Corps each: Right Grand Division (commanded by Major General Edwin V. Sumner; 2nd and 9th Corps) Left Grand Division (commanded by Major General William B. Franklin; 1st and 6th Corps) Center Grand Division (commanded by Major General Joseph Hooker; 3rd and 5th Corps).

22 Catton, THE CIVIL WAR, 271.

23 Joshua Lawrence Chamberlain, BAYONET FORWARD My Civil War Reminiscences (Gettysburg, Pennsylvania: Stan Clark Military Books, 1994) 2; See Catton, THE CIVIL WAR (*Valor and Blunders Produce Fredericksburg's Carnage*)

24 See Catton, THE CIVIL WAR.

25 Trulock, In the Hands of Providence, 97.

* Longstreet's artillery chief was Edward Porter Alexander.

26 Chamberlain, BAYONET FORWARD, 6-7.

27 Ibid., 7.

28 Wallace, Soul Of The Lion, 54.

29 Chalbmberlain, BAYONET FORWARD, 9. (*My Story Of Fredericksburg*)

30 Ibid., 9.

31 Ibid., 10.

32 Trulock, In the Hands of Providence, 100.

* In her notes, Trulock states that this scene describing the Northern lights by Chamberlain was cut by an editor at Cosmopolitan Magazine, from Chamberlain's My Story of Fredericksburg. As it was unusual for the aurora borealis to appear that far south at that time of year, the editor questioned its occurrence. However, other accounts of its appearance were also recorded by a number of soldiers, Major Jedediah Hotchkiss among them.

33 Chamberlain, BAYONET FORWARD, 11. (*My Story Of Fredericksburg*).

34 Ibid., 11 & 12.

35 Ibid., 14 (dialog quoted as is, asides by author).

 * There has been recent controversy over whether General Hooker was actually the officer that Chamberlain talked with. That Chamberlain had only been in the army for three months is a plausible reason for him to have been mistaken. However, as an officer, it seems unlikely that he would not be able to recognized his own Division commander, or that he would identify him as such in an article that could have been disputed by other soldiers who were present. It should be noted however, that Hooker was already deceased when the piece was published.

36 Catton, THE CIVIL WAR, 281.

37 Robert Hunt Rhodes, All For The Union, 97.

38 See Trulock, In the Hands of Providence; See Pullen, The Twentieth Maine.

39 See Catton, THE CIVIL WAR (under *The South's Last Opportunity* 291-295).

40 Trulock, In the Hands of Providence, 110; See Catton, THE CIVIL WAR.

41 Catton, THE CIVIL WAR, 297.(quote); See Pullen, The Twentieth Maine; See Trulock, In the Hands of Providence; See Wallace, Soul Of The Lion.

42 See Catton, THE CIVIL WAR (under *The South's Last Opportunity*).

43 Pullen, The Twentieth Maine, 75.

44 Wallace, Soul Of The Lion, 67.

45 Geoffrey C. Ward, Ric Burns, Ken Burns, The Civil War: An Illustrated History (New York; Knopf, 1990), 210; See Canton, THE CIVIL WAR.

46 Wallace, Soul Of The Lion, 67.

47 See Trulock, In the Hands of Providence; (quote) Chamberlain, Through Blood & Fire At Gettysburg, 11.

 * On behalf of the men from the 2nd Maine, Chamberlain wrote to Maine's governor Abner Coburn on three separate occasions, but his efforts were to no avail.

48 Chamberlain, Through Blood & Fire At Gettysburg, 11; See Pullen, The Twentieth Maine.

 * For an in-depth explanation of why the 2nd Maine men rebelled, see John J. Pullen's book, The Twentieth Maine, pages 77-81 and Thomas Desjardin's book Stand Firm Ye Boys From Maine, pages 16-17..

49 Johnson, Great Battles of THE CIVIL WAR Northern Victories, 33; See Catton, THE CIVIL WAR.

50 See Catton, THE CIVIL WAR (under *The South's Last Opportunity*); See Johnson, Great Battles of THE CIVIL WAR Northern Victories (under *Gettysburg*)

51 See National Park Service U.S. Department of the Interior, Gettysburg Official Map and Guide; See Mark Nesbitt, Ghosts of Gettysburg (Gettysburg Penn.: Thomas Publications, 1991); See Catton, THE CIVIL WAR.

 * Gettysburg was settled in 1780 and was named after Ames Getty.

 * Although Hooker had failed at Chancellorsville, he had shown great skill in the seven weeks since. In the days leading up to Gettysburg he had marched his army hard, putting 100,000 soldiers between Lee and the Union's capitol without Lee even knowing it. However, the animosity between Hooker and Washington (especially with General Halleck) proved to be too much and "Fighting Joe" resigned. General George Meade replaced Hooker on June 28, 1863, becoming the Army of the Potomac's fifth commander in less than a year.

52   Vincent J. Coffey, Turning Points in American History THE BATTLE OF GETTYSBURG (Morristown, New Jersey: Silver Burdett Company) 25.

53 Johnson, Great Battles of THE CIVIL WAR Northern Victories, 38.

* Many, including General Meade, believed that General John Reynolds should have replaced Hooker when Hooker resigned.

54 See Catton, THE CIVIL WAR; See Coffey, THE BATTLE OF GETTYSBURG; See Johnson, Great Battles of THE CIVIL WAR.

55 See Pullen, The Twentieth Maine; (quote) Trulock, In the Hands of Providence, 117.

* Pullen gives a list of the number of miles the 20th marched before reaching Gettysburg: June 26: 20 miles; June 27: 20 miles; June 29: 18 miles; June 30: 23 miles; July 1: 26 miles.

56 See Catton, THE CIVIL WAR; See Johnson, Great Battles of THE CIVIL WAR Northern Victories; Glenn Tucker, Lee and Longstreet at Gettysburg (Indianapolis, Kanas City, New York: The Bobbs-Merrill Company, 1968).

57 Catton, THE CIVIL WAR, 327.

58 Shelby Foote, The Civil War A Narrative Vol 2 Fredericksburg to Meridian, Stars in Their Courses (New York: Random House, 1963), 496

* Near the Trostle farm, Sickles' right leg was almost completely severed when he was hit by a shell. Having used a saddle strap for a tourniquet, he was carried from the field, puffing on a cigar to squelch the spreading rumors that he was dead. Sickles' leg had to be amputated and he donated it to the Army Medical Museum in Washington D.C. where it still can be seen. After the war Sickles used to visit the museum and the leg that used to be his.

59 Ibid., 496.

60 Oliver Willcox Norton, The Attack and Defense of Little Round Top (Gettysburg, Penn.: Stan Clark Military Books, reprinted 1992; first copyright by Norton, 1913) 309.

* This passage by Warren was taken from his letter written to Captain Porter Farley, dated July 13, 1872.

* Having been Meade's Chief Engineer, Warren was already familiar with the Round Tops and knew their importance, thus his discovery that they had been abandoned by Union troops had to have come as a shock.

* In the letter to Captain Farley, Warren said when he saw the glistening gun barrels, which revealed Hood's division hiding in the woods off the Emmittsburg road, "the discovery was intensely thrilling to my feelings and most appalling." [Ibid., 309]

* At the time of the battle, Oliver Willcox Norton, author of The Attack and Defense of Little Round Top, was the bugler and bearer of the headquarters flag for Strong Vincent's 3rd

Brigade, which put him in an excellent position for witnessing what went on. Norton's work is reinforced by all the data he collected; official reports, letters from Warren, accounts by historians, and notably by officers who took part in the battle--Sykes, the commander of the 5th Corps, etc. The authority of this work is valuable, and to Norton's credit, it has withstood the test of time.

Another source of valuable information is Maine At Gettysburg, (Portland, Maine; Lakeside Press Engravers, Printers, and Binders, 1898). This book includes the involvement of all Maine regiments at Gettysburg; the section dealing with the 20th Maine runs from page 249-288. The report on the 20th Maine was prepared by a committee of officers who had fought at Gettysburg, which included Chamberlain, Ellis Spear, and others. Besides recording the events of that day, the report provides a list of men who fought, and also includes a list of those who were killed or wounded.

61 See Norton, The Attack and Defense of Little Round Top.

* Through an aide, Warren sent word to General Meade of the situation, asking him for troops.   Aides, Lieutenants Mackenzie and Reese where then sent to Sykes and Sickles requesting help. Sickles said he could not spare any troops, Sykes said he could spare a brigade and sent word off to General Barnes, commander of the 1st Division. Barnes couldn't be found, and Strong Vincent intercepted the orders. Vincent, who immediately understood the importance of getting Little Round Top manned, did not waste time going through the proper channels for orders; rather, he took it upon himself to get his brigade up to its valuable position on Little Round Top. Thus, as Chamberlain himself stated: "I regard the timely occupation of that position, which was at that stage of the battle the key of the Union defense, as due to the energy and skill of Colonel Vincent." [Ibid., 227]

62 Maine At Gettysburg, Report of Maine Commissioners Prepared by The Executive Committee (Portland, Maine; The Lakeside Press Engravers, Printers and Binders, 1898) 253.

63 Chamberlain, Through Blood & Fire At Gettysburg, 9.

64 See Norton, The Attack and Defense of Little Round Top (under *The War Between the Union and the Confederacy*, also under Oates' Official Report); See Styple, With a Flash of His Sword, (under *Gettysburg, The Battle on the Right* by Col. William C. Oates); See Wallace, Soul Of The Lion.

* Although Oates was the commander for the 15th Alabama, he also had temporary command of the 47th Alabama (for explanation see Norton). One factor that worked against Oates and his men, was thirst--the canteens of the 15th Alabama were dry; at the top of Big Round Top, while the regiments rested, he sent off some men to fill canteens, but they never made it back and were most likely captured.

65 Chamberlain, Through Blood & Fire At Gettysburg, 10; See Pullen, The Twentieth Maine.

* Chamberlain in his official report says "at all hazards"; later he would refer to it as "at all costs"; both imply the same thing.

   * Vincent originally had the 16th Michigan on the left of the 20th Maine; shortly before the battle began he moved that regiment to the right of the 44th New York.

66 Chamberlain, Through Blood & Fire At Gettysburg, 11 & 12.

   * Chamberlain said in his official report that he went into the fight with 386 men in his ranks including 28 officers--of that number, 358 had guns. According to the list given in the report on the 20th in Maine At Gettysburg, [page 263-270] the number of men was higher. Not counting men on special duty or detached service, but including musicians, I tallied 42 men from Company A; 44, Co. B; 51, Co. C; 46, Co. D; 45, Co. E; 58, Co. F; 54, Co. G; 47, Co. H; 55, Co. I; 55, Co. K; plus a Field Staff of 11. Although the total was 508 men and officers, several factors have to be considered. According to the report, the regiment had marched 59 miles from Frederick City to Gettysburg in two days and one night of marching [Pullen gauges the march as being 67 miles] During that time it was not unlikely that a number of soldiers fell out due to illness or fatigue, which was a common occurrence. Another factor in the list, was soldiers who were involved in non-combat duty, medics, cooks, orderlies, baggage carriers, ect. Considering these factors, and excluding Company B's 44 men, who had been sent forward as skirmishes, Chamberlain probably had an estimated 400 men along the crest of Little Round Top at the time of the battle, which wasn't too far off his reported number.

   * Colonel Oates estimated he had 700 men in his 15th Alabama Regiment. Oates also had temporary command of the 47th Alabama but this added force of a hundred or so men was not very effective during the conflict [a number of companies in the 47th broke early in the battle and retreated up Big Round Top]

   * Although Colonel Oates had the advantage of more men, he also had the disadvantage of having to charge uphill.

67 Chamberlain, Through Blood & Fire At Gettysburg, 14.

   *   Law's line, running in order from its right to left, consisted of the following regiments:15th, 47th, 4th Alabama, 5th, 4th Texas, 48th, 44th Alabama.

68 Ibid., 15.

69 Styple, With a Flash of His Sword, 54 (under *Gettysburg, The Battle on the Right* by Col. William C. Oates)

70 Pullen, The Twentieth Maine, 118.

71 Styple, With a Flash of His Sword, 55 (under *Gettysburg, The Battle on the Right* by Col. William C. Oates)

72 Styple, With a Flash of His Sword, 67 (taken from the account given by Theodore Gerrish, Company H, 20th Maine)

73 Chamberlain, Through Blood & Fire At Gettysburg, 17.

74 Ibid., 17.

75 See Chamberlain, Through Blood & Fire At Gettysburg; See Trulock, In the Hands of Providence.

76 Chamberlain, Through Blood &Fire At Gettysburg, 20; See Trulock, In the Hands of

Providence.
    77 Ibid., 16.
    *   When Colonel Stockton resigned, shortly after the Battle of Chancellorsville, Strong
Vincent, who was only twenty-six, was put in command of the 3rd Brigade. Although Vincent
had already proven his abilities as an officer, his promotion to brigadier general did not occur
until he was unconscious and dying. His death, five days after being wounded at Little Round
Top, deeply saddened Chamberlain. The two had been close friends and to Fannie, Joshua
wrote, "I grieve for him much." [Trulock, In the Hands of Providence, 160] After the war,
Chamberlain "did many acts of kindness" for Vincent's "impoverished widow." [Wallace, Soul
Of The Lion, 70]
    78 Ibid, 16; See Norton, The Attack and Defense of Little Round Top.
    *   A moving account of O'Rorke's death was given by Captain Farley of the 140th New York
Volunteers, who accompanied O'Rorke's body back to the surgeons station. Although this is
a lengthy excerpt, I feel it gives an inside look at the camaraderie of soldiers; and the respect
due to O'Rorke :
    "... He had fallen instantly dead. A bloody froth on the side of his neck showed the fatal
track of the bullet. Up to that time in my life I had never felt a grief so sharply, nor realized
the significance of death so well, as then, when the wild excitement of our fight was over and
I saw O'Rorke lying there so pale and peaceful. To me and all of us he had seemed so near the
beau ideal of a soldier and a gentleman, all that he had been and the bright promise of what he
was to be, was so fresh in our minds, and now, in an instant, the fatal bullet had cut short the
chapter of that fair life. I choked with grief as I stood beside his lifeless form. I had known
and loved him well, and in these last few weeks better than ever, my position as his adjutant
naturally leading to intercourse of the most familiar kind, as day by day we ate our soldier's fare
together and often at night slept with the same blanket covering us. For him to die was to me
like losing a brother, and that brother almost the perfection of the manly graces. What a blow
was such a death to the young wife and loving family who far away waited for the news from
Gettysburg; what was it to us of the regiment whose fortunes he had shared, whose wants and
welfare he had watched over, and who had been the witnesses of the last gallant effort of his life
when inspiring everyone who heard him with an enthusiasm which only master minds can
impart, he started his men with their empty muskets full in the face of a withering fire and
springing to their front in the wild 'rapture of the strife' fell dead among them.
    It was only natural that his so sudden death should most deeply affect us. But time and
place alike forbade the comfort which comes to the heart when it yields to its grief.
    I took from his pockets his watch and some trifles, pulled from his hands the long gloves
which he had worn and slipped them in his belt, helped compose his supple form in fitting way,
collected the men who had brought him and others to the surgeon's station, and taking a last
look at poor O'Rorke went back to the regiment." Norton, The Attack and Defense of Little
Round Top, 139-140]

79 Shelby Foote, Vol 2 Fredericksburg to Meridian, 504.

80 Ibid., 504.

* This was said by noted Civil War author, Shelby Foote.

81 Styple, With a Flash of His Sword, 55 (under *Gettysburg, The Battle on the Right*, by Col. William C. Oates; See Norton, The Attack and Defense of Little Round Top.

* Oates' brother was captured and died of his wounds 23 days after the battle.

82 See Ibid.

83 Chamberlain, Through Blood & Fire At Gettysburg, 21.

* Wallace says that with "sixty rounds to a man they had expended more than twenty thousand bullets"

84 Styple, With a Flash of His Sword, 56. (under Oates account)

85 Chamberlain, Through Blood & Fire At Gettysburg, 22.

86 Ibid., 23.

* There was some controversy about whether the 20th hesitated before making their charge but in Chamberlain's address at the dedication of the monument on Little Round Top, he said: "That is not so. No man hesitated. There might be an appearance of it to those who did not understand the whole situation. The left wing went back like an ox-bow, or sharp lunette, had to take some time to come up into the line of our general front, so as to form the close, continuous edge which was to strike like a sword-cut upon the enemy's ranks. By the time they got up and straightened the line, the center and salient, you may be sure, was already in motion. Nobody hesitated to obey the order. In fact, to tell the truth, the order was never given, or but imperfectly. The enemy were already pressing up the slope. There was only time or need for the words, "Bayonet! Forward to the right!" The quick witted and tense-nerved men caught the words out of my lips and almost the action out of my hands. . . .So much in elucidation of facts. You see there may be stories apparently not consistent with each other, yet all of them true in their time and place, and so far as each actor is concerned." [Styple, With a Flash of His Sword, 123].

87 Styple, With a Flash of His Sword, 69. (account given by Theodore Gerrish of Company H, 20th Maine)

88 Norton, The Attack and Defense of Little Round Top, 215 (under Chamberlain's official report; July 6, 1863).

* In Chamberlain's official report written three days after the battle, he stated: "Holding fast by our right, and swinging forward with our left, we made an extended 'right wheel,' before which the enemy's second line broke and fell back." There has been some controversy as to whether the order for a "right wheel" was ever actually made. Whether it was or not, the action of a 'right wheel' was definitely carried out when the left wing swung around the base of the slope to join their advancing front on the right. It is interesting to note that in his official report Chamberlain puts 'right wheel' in quotes, as though denoting a difference between a right wheel executed on a parade ground, and the action of what occurred on that rocky slope. It should also be noted that in this report he never stated that he ordered a right wheel.

89 Pullen, The Twentieth Maine, 124.

* This was said by an officer from the 83rd Pennsylvania.

90 Styple, With a Flash of His Sword, 69. (Under Gerrish account)

* Oates' losses had been heavy, and believing he was being attack at both his front, flanks, and right rear, he gave a signal for retreat, but not all of his officers or men got word of it, and when the final charge was made by the 20th Maine seconds later, Oates' order only added to the confusion, some Rebels retreating, some charging, some surrendering on the spot.

91 Styple, With a Flash of His Sword, 69. (Under Gerrish account)

92 Styple, With a Flash of His Sword, 57. (under Oates account); See Pullen, The Twentieth Maine; See Wallace, Soul Of The Lion.

* Oates' men retreated toward both Big Round Top and the Weikert Farm Lane. Although Oates says in his account that in their retreat they broke through a line of dismounted cavalrymen, he was mistaken. There were no cavalrymen in the area (see Norton, page 112); one explanation is that Oates mistook Morrill's Company B for cavalrymen.

93 See Styple, With a Flash of His Sword, (under Morrill's official report)

* 12 or 15 sharpshooters from the 2nd U.S.S.S. who had earlier been run off of Big Round Top by Oates, joined Morrill and his men at the stone wall--these men would be responsible for the mysterious fire that Oates experienced from the right rear.

94 Chamberlain, Through Blood & Fire At Gettysburg, 25.

95 See Chamberlain, Through Blood & Fire At Gettysburg; See Pullen, The Twentieth Maine; See Trulock, In the Hands of Providence; See Norton, The Attack and Defense of Little Round Top.

* The officer who fired at Chamberlain was Lt. Wicker of the 15th Alabama Regiment. Some accounts say he fired and missed, other's say his gun misfired.   In his official report, Chamberlain refers to the gun as a "Colts" revolver and recorded that "An officer fired his pistol at my head.."

96 Styple, With a Flash of His Sword, 134. (under Melcher's account).

97 Ibid., 57 (Oates, Battle on the Right)

98 Norton, The Attack and Defense of Little Round Top, 215 first quote; 217 second quote. (Chamberlain's official report)

99 Trulock, In the Hands of Providence, 155.

100 Ibid., 154.

101 Styple, With a Flash of His Sword, 58. (under Oates' account)

102 Chamberlain, Through Blood & Fire At Gettysburg, 26.

103 Wallace, Soul Of The Lion, 104.

104 Chamberlain, Through Blood & Fire At Gettysburg, 27-28.

Notes on Part Three

1* The inscription on the monument on top of Big Round Top reads as follows:

THE 20th MAINE REG'T.
3^D BRIG, 1ST DIV. 5TH CORPS
COLONEL
JOSHUA L. CHAMBERLAIN
CAPTURED AND HELD THIS
POSITION ON THE EVENING
OF JULY 2^D 1863, PURSUING
THE ENEMY FROM ITS FRONT
ON THE LINE MARKED BY
ITS MONUMENT BELOW
THE REG'T LOST IN BATTLE
130 KILLED AND WOUNDED
OUT OF 358 ENGAGED
THIS MONUMENT MARKS THE
EXTREME LEFT OF THE UNION
LINE DURING THE BATTLE OF
THE 3^D DAY

2 Trulock, In the Hands of Providence, 151.
3 Styple, With a Flash of His Sword, 44-45. (under Chamberlain's official report: written in the field near Emmittsburg, on July 6th, 1863; See Norton, The Attack and Defense of Little Round Top.
4 SeeThomas A Desjardin, Stand Firm Ye Boys From Maine (Gettysburg, Pa.: Thomas Publications, 1995).
5 Johnson, Great Battles of THE CIVIL WAR Northern Victories, 49; See Catton, THE CIVIL WAR.
6 Gettysburg, (Gettysburg, Pennsylvania: Tem Inc.), 18. (Informational Booklet, no author given).
7 Coffey, The Battle Of Gettysburg, 53.
*   The breakthrough at the stone wall is referred to as the "high-water mark of the Confederacy" because this was the closest the Confederates came to penetrating the Union line that day, and the closest they would come in winning the war. The "high-water mark" is considered by most historians as the turning point in the war.
8 Catton, THE CIVIL WAR, 344.

* Another devasting blow to the South that day was the fall of Vicksburg. At about the same time Pickett's Charge was being made in Gettysburg, Confederate General John Pemberton and an acquaintance from the old army, General Ulysses S. Grant, were sitting together on a Vicksburg hillside, discussing the terms of the city's surrender. In Gettysburg, the North had won a great battle, but with the fall of Vicksburg, they strategically won the war. With Vicksburg and the Mississippi in the Union's possession, the South had been severed.

9 Catton, THE CIVIL WAR, 247.

10 Ibid., 423.

* The general from whom the quote was taken was Union general Ben Butler.

11 African Americans VOICES of TRIUMPH Perseverance (Alexandria, Virginia: Time-Life Books, 1993) 60.

* Frederick Douglass: Born as a slave on a Maryland plantation in 1817, Douglass, whose given name was Frederick Augustus Washington Bailey, was taught to read and write as a boy by the wife of one of his owners. Having suffered the turmoil of slavery throughout his childhood, Douglass escaped to New York at twenty-one, disguised as a sailor. After his well-known book, Narrative of the Life of Frederick Douglass, an American Slave, was published in 1845, Douglass fled to Europe to avoid being captured and returned to his former owner. In England, he was well received as a writer and speaker, and when he decided to return to America, Britons raised money to pay for his freedom. Back in the States, Douglass started the newspaper, North Star, an antislavery weekly. He not only became active in the underground railroad, but through his newspaper and speeches, became one of the leading voices for his race in America. Throughout his life his dedication and powerful writings would help to promote the issues of human rights. On February 20, 1895, this remarkable man who had once written to his former owner to say, "I am your fellow man but not your slave," died of a heart attack just hours after giving a speech on women's rights. Of his death, Robert Smalls (black congressman and war hero) said, "The greatest of the race has fallen." [Ibid., 60]

12 Trulock, In the Hands of Providence, 163.

* This was quoted from a private in Company H, 20th Maine.

13 Ibid., 208.

14 See Wallace, Soul Of The Lion.

* Captain Walter Morrill and fifty volunteers from the 20th Maine joined in a night attack with the 6th Corps against the enemy's main works near Kelly's Ford. Outnumbered and under intense fire, the Union soldiers managed to overtake the entrenched Confederates, capturing "four guns, over 1,700 men (including 130 officers), two brigade commanders, and eight battle flags." [Trulock, In the Hands of Providence, 173]

* For his "dash and gallantry" in leading his men in this attack, Morrill received the Congressional Medal of Honor for action on November 7, 1863: Besides Chamberlain and Morrill, two other men from the 20th Maine would receive the Congressional Medal of Honor--Andrew Tozier for action on July 2, 1863, and Albert Fernald for action on April 1, 1865.

15 See Trulock, In the Hands of Providence; See Wallace, Soul Of The Lion.

16 Styple, With a Flash of His Sword, 169. (under *An Experience In The Battle Of The Wilderness*, by Brevet-Major Holman S. Melcher); See Catton, THE CIVIL WAR; See Trulock, In the Hands of Providence.

17 Catton, THE CIVIL WAR, 446; See Trulock, In the Hands of Providence; See Wallace, Soul Of The Lion.

18 Trulock, In the Hands of Providence, 180; See Styple, With a Flash of His Sword, (under *An Experience In the Battle Of The Wilderness*, by Holman S. Melcher)

19 Description of Charlemagne obtained from the Chamberlain files at the Pejepscot Historical Society, original in the collection of the University of Maine at Orono.

* On a sheet of U.S. Customs Service stationery, Chamberlain described Charlemagne and their relationship. Charlemagne, who had a white diamond on his forehead and one white sock on a hind leg, had been captured from the Confederates in the Shenandoah Valley. The bond between Joshua and his horse was extremely close; Charlemagne used to stand by Joshua's tent as though he were a guard dog waiting for his master to emerge. Although Joshua, on occasion, let other soldiers ride his horse, he said that Charlemagne always came back from the mission first. Spirited in battle, Charlemagne sometimes took Chamberlain places where Joshua said he had no business being. The horse was shot three times in battle, and after all they had been through together, Joshua could not have left his friend behind after the war. Charlemagne was brought home to Brunswick where he became the "idolized" family pet and "playmate" for Chamberlain's children. When Charlemagne died, Joshua gave his faithful friend a Christian burial at Domhegan, the Chamberlain's ocean home in Brunswick.

20 Trulock, In the Hands of Providence, 193 & 194.

21 Styple, With a Flash of His Sword, 274; See Trulock, In the Hands of Providence.

22 Trulock, In the Hands of Providence, (both quotes) 194.

23 Ibid., 105.I

24 See Wallace, Soul Of The Lion; See Trulock, In the Hands of Providence; See Pullen, The Twentieth Maine; See, article in Chamberlain's file at the Pejepscot Historical Society--Gov. Chamberlain our next U.S. Senator, 1870.

25 Trulock, In the Hands of Providence, 203 & 204.

26 Chamberlain, Bayonet! Forward, 48. (under *Reminiscences of Petersburg and Appomattox*)

27 Wallace, Soul Of The Lion, 132.

* As a means of communication, flags were used on the fields to identify troops and the whereabouts of their commanders. The flag for the 1st Div., 5th Corps was triangular-shaped, had a white background, and in the center, a red Maltese cross. After the war, Chamberlain had a Maltese cross engraved in stone and painted the appropriate colors. The stone was placed on the outside of the front chimney. Although the chimney no longer exists, the stone was preserved and can be seen at his museum in Brunswick.

28 Chamberlain, Bayonet! Forward, (both quotes) 48. (under Reminiscences of Petersburg and Appomattox)

29 Trulock, In the Hands of Providence, 212.

30 See Ibid; See Wallace, Soul Of The Lion; See The Medical and Surgical History of the War Of The Rebellion Part 2, Vol. 2 (Washington: Government Printing Office, 1878), Case number 1056.

* The description of Chamberlain's wound in this case history is described as followed: "the ball entered the right hip in front of and a little below the right trochanter major, passed diagonally backward, and made exit above and posteriorly to the left trochanter. The bladder was involved in the wound at some portion. . ."

* During Trulock's research she consulted William H. Annesly, Jr. M.D. and his description reads as followed: "Projectile entered anterior and below the right presumed greater trochanter and passed upward through the bladder and emerged in the rear of the left acetabulum."

* In the pension examiner's report made in September of 1873, he states Chamberlain "very often suffers severe pain," and classified Chamberlain's disability as "total."

31 Trulock, In the Hands of Providence, 215: a copy of this letter is on display at the Chamberlain Museum in Brunswick.

32 Ibid., 215.

33 See Wallace, Soul Of The Lion; See Trulock, In the Hands of Providence.

34 Johnson, Great Battles of THE CIVIL WAR Northern Victories, 64.

35 See Catton for statistics, THE CIVIL WAR, 519; See Wallace, Soul Of The Lion; See Trulock, In the Hands of Providence.

36 Trulock, In the Hands of Providence, 225.

37 Chamberlain, The Passing of the Armies, 46.

38 Ibid., 46.

39 Ibid., 48.

40 Ibid., 48.

41 Ibid., 50.

42 Ibid., 56. (statistics--pages 53 & 54: Chamberlain said they fought the Confederate brigades of Gracie, Ransom, Wallace, and Wise under command of General R. H. Anderson; by their last morning report, the men of these troops listed "effective" for the field was 6,277.

43 Ibid., 56.

44 Ibid., 73; See Trulock, In the Hands of Providence.

45 Ibid., 76.

* Because of the introduction of better rifles, the commanders in the Civil War had to adapt new techniques of warfare on the battlefield. In previous wars, soldiers had to be at close range

in order to fight and relied heavily on the bayonet; they also went into battle in column formations. Because weapon technology had advanced, these latter tactics no longer worked, and their usage produced tremendous casualties. Through experience, Chamberlain was well aware of this and thus sent his men across the open field in loose formation. This guerrilla-like fashion, allowed the men the freedom to run and dodge their way across open areas, making them harder targets, and thus reducing casualties. With the introduction of the machine gun in War World One, this technique was common for the same reasons.

46 Wallace, Soul Of The Lion, 155; See Trulock, In the Hands of Providence.

47 Chamberlain, The Passing Of The Armies, 76.

48 Trulock, In the Hands of Providence, 235 (first quote); 273 (second quote).

49 Ibid., 299 & 300.

50 Chamberlain, The Passing Of The Armies, 237.

51 Ibid., both quotes taken from 238.

52 Ibid., 240.

* Chamberlain later said that when he saw that the soldier's flag of truce was a white towel, he had wondered where, in either dirty army, someone could have found one.

53 Chamberlain, The Passing Of The Armies, 246 & 247.

54 Trulock, In the Hands of Providence, 300.

55 Ibid., 303.

56 Chamberlain, The Passing Of The Armies, 260.

57 Chamberlain, The Passing Of The Armies, 261.

58 Ibid., 260.

59 Trulock, In the Hands of Providence, 305.

60 Catton, THE CIVIL WAR, 592.

61 See Ibid.

62 Chamberlain, Bayonet! Forward, 257. (under *One Hundredth Anniversary of the Birth of Abraham Lincoln*)

63 Ibid., 258.

64 Geoffrey Ward, Ric Burns, Ken Burns, THE CIVIL WAR (New York; Vintage Civil War Library, 1990) 294-295.

65 Catton, THE CIVIL WAR, 603.

* On May 4th, 1865, President Lincoln was buried in Springfield, Illinois.

66 Chamberlain, The Passing Of The Armies, 278.

67 Ibid., 282 & 283.

68 Ibid., 283.

69 Trulock, In the Hands of Providence, 333.

70 Chamberlain, The Passing Of The Armies, 391 & 392.

Notes on Part Four

1 Wallace, Soul Of The Lion, 223.

* William DeWitt Hyde, was Chamberlain's Latin tutor before Joshua attended Bowdoin as a student. Hyde later became President of Bowdoin (after Chamberlain). Hyde held Joshua in high regard and gave a lengthy eulogy at Chamberlain's funeral.

2 Joshua Lawrence Chamberlain Museum, (pamphlet put out by the Pejepscot Historical Society) back cover; See Trulock, In the Hands of Providence.

* General Grant and his wife were guests of the Chamberlain's during Bowdoin's commencement ceremonies in August of 1865. As this was directly after the war, Grant's presence in the small town of Brunswick caused quite a stir.

3 See Trulock, In the Hands of Providence.

4 Ibid., 349; second quote, Wallace, Soul Of The Lion, 33.

5 See Trulock, In the Hands of Providence.

6 See Wallace, Soul Of The Lion; for statistics page 207.

7 See Ibid.

* The 13th Amendment abolished slavery in the United States; the 14th Amendment gave former slaves the rights of citizenship--the right to vote; the 15th Amendment strengthened the former Amendment, and states in Section 1:"The right of citizens of the United States to vote shall not be denied or abridged by the United States or by any State on account of race, color, or previous condition of servitude."

8 Wallace, Soul Of The Lion, 205.

9 Ibid., 206.

10 Joshua Chamberlain, Governor Chamberlain's Address, 1870 (Augusta: Sprague, Owen & Nash, printers to the State) 12; See Wallace, Soul Of The Lion.

11 Ibid., 20.

12 Ibid., 16.

13 Joshua Chamberlain, Governor Chamberlain's Address, 1867 (Augusta: Stevens & Sayward, printers to the State) 13.

14 Wallace, Soul Of The Lion, 208.

15 Ibid., 209.

16 Ibid., 213.

17 See Ellis Paxson Oberholtzer, History of the United States since The Civil War, Vol. 2 (New York: MacMillan Company, 1928)

* The accusation that President Johnson was involved in the plot to assassinate Lincoln was ridiculous, as he was one of the intended victims. According to Booth's plan, George Atzerodt

was suppose to kill Andrew Johnson; while David Herold and Lewis Paine, were ordered to kill Secretary of State William Seward.

* "Radical Republicans"--were a group of Republicans that felt Lincoln's reconstruction plan, which Johnson was trying to put into action, was too lenient. These power-hungry Congressmen led by Thaddeus Stevens wanted Congress and not the President to decide how the South was to be dealt with, and were willing to unjustly impeach their president in order to get their way.

18 Ibid., 72.

19 Wallace, Soul Of The Lion, 215.

20 Ibid., 215.

21 See Trial of Andrew Joshnson Vol. 1 (Washington: Government Printing Office, 1868); See Wallace, Soul Of The Lion; See Paxson, History of the United States.

* William Pitt Fessenden was born in Boscawen, New Hampshire in 1806. After graduating from Bowdoin College in 1823, he went on to become a lawyer. A Republican, he served several years in the Maine House of Representatives and for fifteen years was a United States senator. During the war he acted as Secretary of the Treasury. Fessenden was well respected in Washington and had a reputation as an excellent debater. A year after voting "not guilty" at President Johnson's impeachment trial, Senator Fessenden died at the age of 63.

22 Evening Post, newspaper article about Governor Chamberlain, Sept. 1869; found in the Chamberlain Files; Pejepscot Historical Society.

23 Governor Chamberlain's Address, (1868) 13.

24 Evening Post, newspaper article about Governor Chamberlain, Sept. 1869; See Wallace, Soul Of The Lion.

25 Wallace, Soul Of The Lion, 214.

* In January of 1835 Joseph Sager was hanged for murdering his wife (he poisoned her with arsenic): from that time on, only one other murderer would be put to death before Chamberlain took office (in 1864, Governor Cony signed the death warrant on Francis Couillard Spencer, who while in prison, killed a warden). The failure of previous governors to set dates of execution for convicted murderers was largely due to the problem of having no time limits placed upon them.   Like Chamberlain, it was an issue a number of former governors had brought to legislation. [See Edward Schriver, New England Quarterly 63, June 1990, 271-287.]

26 Governor Chamberlain's Address, (1868) 12.

27 Governor Chamberlain's Address, (1867) 28.

28 Ibid., 29.

29 Governor Chamberlain's Address, (1869) 9.

30 Ibid., 9.

31 Ibid., 9 & 10.

32 Ibid., 13.

* Clifton Harris, who was from Fortress Monroe, Virginia, had only been in Maine a short

time before murdering Mrs. Susannah Kinsley and her deaf companion, Miss Polly Caswell. Although Harris implicated Luther Verrill as his accomplice, Verrill was never convicted. Harris was hanged on March 12th, 1869 for his crimes.[See Edward Schriver, New England Quarterly 63, June 1990, 271-287.]

33 Evening Post, newspaper article about Governor Chamberlain, Sept. 1869.

34 * Capitol punishment in Maine was first abolished in 1876; seven years later, in 1883, it again became a legal practice in the state. It was abolished a final time in 1887. Daniel Wilkinson, who murdered police officer William Lawrence during a robbery in Bath, was the last person to be executed in Maine for murder. Wilkinson was hanged in November of 1885. [See Schriver, New England Quarterly 63, June 1990, 271-287.]

35 See Wallace, Soul Of The Lion; See Trulock, In the Hands of Providence.

36 Wallace, Soul Of The Lion, 232.

37 See Ibid.; See Trulock, In the Hands of Providence.

38 Trulock, In the Hands of Providence, 344.

39 Wallace, Soul Of The Lion, 232.

40 Ibid., 231 & 232.

41 Ibid., 233

42 Ibid., 234.

43 Trulock, In the Hands of Providence, 345.

44 Ibid., 345.

45 Wallace, Soul Of The Lion, 238; See Trulock, In the Hands of Providence.

* At the Chamberlain Museum in Brunswick, there is an excerpt from a letter written by E.M. Cousins to his mother, dated May 24, 1874. In his letter, Cousins, a Bowdoin Freshman, wrote about the student protest over the military drill.

"...there is a rebellion in Bowdoin against the "Military Drill" in which students are forced to engage. The man who has charge of the drill is very unpopular. An officer in the U.S. army, he treats the students as if they were privates in that army...We are forced to buy uniforms and appear in them...Last week some of the Juniors groaned at the close of their drill...the Faculty dismissed one Junior from the college and suspended five others...The class was naturally indignant and held a meeting and voted to drill no more. The other two classes...voted to cut drill. I should not be surprised if 125 students were suspended."

46 Ibid., 240.

47 Ibid., 240.

48 Trulock, In the Hands of Providence, 347.

49 See Wallace, Soul Of The Lion; Information about Bowdoin during World War Two was given to me by Julia Oehmig--Curator, Pejepscot Historical Society; Information about women being admitted to Bowdoin was furnished by Susan Kimbal--reference department, Bowdoin Library.

50 Wallace, Soul Of The Lion, 252; See Trulock, In the Hands of Providence.

51 Ibid., 256; See Trulock, In the Hands of Providence; See Fred Humiston, "Twelve Days That Shook Maine," newspaper article, Portland Press Herald, Aug. 20, 1961.

* For an in-depth account of Chamberlain's involvement during the 12 Day Revolt, see Wallace, Soul Of The Lion, 253-273.

* Lot Morrill encouraged Garcelon to let the State Supreme Court decide the matter involving the House and Senate. Chamberlain agreed with Morrill, and in a letter he sent to Garcelon, Joshua urged Garcelon to heed Morrill's advice which he considered "eminently wise."

* James G. Blaine, was born in Pennsylvania in 1830. After graduating from Washington College, he taught school for a time in Kentucky and Philadelphia. Blaine married Harriet Stanwood, also a teacher. The couple eventually moved to Maine, where Harriet had grown up and where her family still resided. Blaine, who was a good writer, bought the *Kennebec Journal* with Joseph Baker and for a number of years wrote and edited. The *Journal* had a wide audience and Blaine's articles soon became popular. His career in politics began at the age of twenty-eight when he was elected to the State legislature in 1858. Ambitious and articulate, Blaine rapidly moved up the political ladder, eventually running for Presidency in the 1884 election, which he lost to Grover Cleveland by a close margin. Blaine died in 1893, and his beautiful mansion in Augusta was given to the State by his daughter, in memory of Blaine's grandson who had been killed in World War I. The Blaine Mansion serves as the home for Maine governors. [See Harold B. Clifford, Maine and Her People (Freeport, Maine: The Bond Wheelwright Company, 1957); See James W. North, The History Of Augusta Maine (Somersworth, New Hampshire: New England History Press, 1981)]

52 Wallace, Soul Of The Lion, 259.

53 Fred Humiston, "Twelve Days That Shook Maine."

54 Wallace, Soul Of The Lion, 259.

55 Ibid., 260.

56 See Ibid.

57 Ibid., 267; See Trulock, In the Hands of Providence.

58 Wallace, Soul Of The Lion, 264.

59 Ibid., 264.

60 Trulock, In the Hands of Providence, 358.

61 Wallace, Soul Of The Lion, 264.

62 Ibid., 264.

63 Ibid., 265.

64 Ibid., 265 & 266.

65 Ibid., 266.

66 Ibid., 268.

67 Trulock, In the Hands of Providence, 357.

68 Wallace, Soul Of The Lion, 247. This was said by Bowdoin President William DeWitt Hyde.

* Trulock's book, In the Hands of Providence, gives another factor which played into Chamberlain's resignation. The author writes that Joshua "felt that his political enemies in influential positions would act against the best interests of Bowdoin as long as he stayed at its head." [Trulock, In the Hands of Providence, 362.]

* Although Joshua was offered presidencies at three other colleges, he turned them down. He served as a member of the Board of Trustees at Bowdoin for forty-seven years.

69 See Wallace, Soul Of The Lion.

70 Trulock, In the Hands of Providence, 367.

71 Wallace, Soul Of The Lion, 279.

72 Trulock, In the Hands of Providence, 367.

73 See Wallace, Soul Of The Lion.

* Joshua's ocean home was once used as a shipyard by its previous owner Israel Simpson. Chamberlain purchased the house, barn, wharf, and five acres of surrounding land after the war. He called his ocean home Domhegan after one of the Native American chiefs who had originally owned the land.

74 "Millitary Order of the Loyal Legion of The United States," *Tribute to the Memory of Joshua Chamberlain*, 12.

* This tribute can be found in both The Passing of the Armies, and "Bayonet! Forward", published by Stan Clark Military Books.

75 Chamberlain, The Passing of the Armies, 56-59.

76 Ibid., back cover.

77 Ibid., 351 & 352.

78 Trulock, In the Hands of Providence, 360 &361.

79 Ibid., 521 (note 77).

* In August of 1896, at the age of fifty-five, Joshua's brother Tom died. His death was brought on by a chronic lung condition and heart disease. Like many soldiers, Tom had struggled in the post-war years. For a time he worked as a clerk in New York, and after his brother John died, he married John's widow. The couple returned to Maine where Tom worked as a merchant. Tom continued to move from one job to the next, and while Joshua was in Florida, he found employment for Tom there. But Tom, who had served his country so well during the war, and even attained the brevet promotion to colonel, had trouble settling down and accepting responsibility for himself and his loving wife, Delia. His restlessness was a continuous worry to his family. Tom and Delia lived apart from each other for extended periods. At one point, because Tom was remiss in supporting her, Delia had to seek financial help from Tom's mother. Yet, when Tom became ill, Delia, who had always been faithful to her husband, was there to nurse him. When Delia died in 1923, she left Brewer Library a sum of

two-hundred dollars in memory of Tom. [See Trulock, In the Hands of Providence]

* Joshua's sister Sae married Charles O. Farrington, a banker and store owner from Brewer. They had three sons who died in infancy, one was named Lawrence Joshua. Their two daughters, Dana and Alice Farrington survived both parents but never had children of their own. [See Trulock, In the Hands of Providence]

80 Newspaper article found in the Chamberlain files at the Pejepscot Historical Society. I was unable to locate the entire article, or the name of the author; from information given in the piece, the writer was a woman who had interviewed Chamberlain in his later years.

81 Chamberlain's early memoirs, Bowdoin Spring/Summer 1991, Vol 64 No. 1, 11.

82 Trulock, In the Hands of Providence, 112-113.

83 Ibid., 361.

84 Ibid., 355.

85 Ibid., 86.

86 Ibid., 163.

87 Ibid., 362.

88 File on Harold Wyllys Chamberlain; Bowdoin College, Special Collections.

* In Wyllys' file, which is listed under his first name, I found a clipping dated 1906, from which the information I used was taken. It is believed to have come from a reunion update of his class of 1881. In this update he says, "I am still a bachelor, though I do not expect to always remain in the state of single cussedness." He also writes, "Bowdoin and the boys of '81 always have a warm corner in my heart."

89 Ibid.

* Wyllys said one of the reasons he returned to Brunswick was his mother's "failing health."

90 Wallace, Soul Of The Lion, 308 & 309.

* Upon his death, Joshua left his estate to his children (Grace recieved property, Wyllys, money). The entire estate was appraised to be $33,608.11. Wallace said that although that was a respectable amount for the times, it was "hardly evidence of conspicuous financial success." [Ibid., 308] Following the death of his brother-in-law, Wyllys lived with his sister Grace and her children until his death in 1928. Grace died nine years later, and both children are buried next to their parents in Pine Grove Cemetery in Brunswick.

91 Ibid., 300.

92 All quotes on bracelet: The Chamberlain Bracelet, Chamberlain files, Pejepscot Historical Society.

93 Trulock, In the Hands of Providence, 370.

94 Ibid., 371.

95 Chamberlain, The Passing of The Armies, 432; Trulock, In the Hands of Providence, 371.

* Although this passage would later be used in The Passing of The Armies, Chamberlain originally wrote it in an address about the last review which was delivered at a meeting for

Maine veterans. Trulock, author of In the Hands of Providence, said that "the homage was placed so that the casual listener or reader would not realize that it was not a part of the description" involving "the women who had nursed the suffering wounded during the war," and that she felt it was really written as a tribute to Fannie. As the piece was composed directly following Fannie's death and is so reflective of their relationship, I believe Trulock's insightful assumption is correct.

* Because of her natural family's history of blindness, and the progressive and painful nature her own disease, Fannie could have suffered from glaucoma.

* Although Reverend Adams and his wife raised Fannie, it is interesting to note that on her gravestone it states she is the daughter of Ashur and Amelia Adams (her natural parents).

96 Wallace, Soul Of The Lion, 292.

97 Trulock, In the Hands of Providence, 372.

98 Ibid., 372; second quote, Wallace, Soul Of The Lion, 306.

99 See Wallace, Soul Of The Lion; See Trulock, In the hands of Providence.

* Chamberlain was involved with a great number of organizations: Trulock lists seventeen in her book, many of which he served as president and vice-president for: American Political Science Association, American Historical Association, and American Bible Society among them.

* Joshua's granddaughter Eleanor would become a lawyer and work for the U.S. State Department in foreign services. Rosamond would earn a graduate degree in social work, "specializing in children's welfare." Beatrice, the youngest, would not attend college; she married David Patten in 1918. None of Joshua's granddaughters had children. [Trulock, In the Hands of Providence, 528.]

100 Ibid., 296.

* Fannie did not accompany Joshua on his trip to Egypt. Because of her blindness, Fannie, who used to love to travel, preferred to stay close to home. While Joshua was away she stayed with Grace and her family in Boston. Like her husband, Fannie took great joy in visiting her grandchildren.

101 Ibid., 296 & 297.

102 Chamberlain, Through Blood & Fire at Gettysburg, 27.

103 Ibid., 28.

104 Wallace, Soul Of The Lion, 307.

105 "Millitary Order of The Loyal Legion of The United States," *Tribute to the Memory of Joshua Chamberlain*, 7.

106 Ibid., 8.

* Eugenie Harward Skolfield Whittier preserved and saved a handful of leaves from Chamberlain's funeral wreath. These were discovered among her things in the Skolfield-Whittier House in Brunswick, Maine. The leaves are on display at The Chamberlain Museum.

Union President

Lincoln, Abraham--Born on February 12, 1809 in a log cabin in the backwoods of Kentucky, Lincoln came from humble beginnings and was no stranger to hard physical work. Preferring to labor with his mind instead of his hands, he struggled to educate himself while undertaking a variety of jobs for financial support, which included working as store clerk, rail-splitter, farm hand, postmaster, surveyor, and operator of a whiskey still. During the Black Hawk war, he served as a captain of militia. Continuing to educate himself, he studied law, eventually becoming a successful prairie lawyer based in Springfield, Illinois. Naturally drawn to politics, in 1834, Lincoln was elected to the Illinois legislature and served four consecutive terms. In 1842, he married Mary Todd whose reputable family were slave owners from Lexington, Kentucky. Elected to Congress, Lincoln served in the House of Representatives from 1847-1849 and, largely due to his criticism of the Mexican War, was limited to one term. Although Lincoln lost the Senate race against Stephen Douglas in 1858, his public debates with Douglas gave him national recognition. During the Republican Convention held in Chicago in May of 1860, Lincoln was nominated for the presidency, and Hannibal Hamlin, who hailed from Maine, was nominated vice-president. Against a divided Democratic party the Republicans won the electoral vote by a landslide in November of 1860. On March 4, 1861, Lincoln was inaugurated in Washington, becoming the 16th president of the United States.

Union Generals

Grant, Ulysses S.--He was born on April 27, 1822 in Point Pleasant, Ohio. His given name was Hiram Ulysses, but upon entering West Point in 1839, he was mistakenly registered as Ulysses Simpson Grant--a circumstance the quiet young cadet chose not to correct. In 1843, Grant graduated from West Point twenty-first in a class of thirty-nine. He served in the regular army for fifteen years and fought in the Mexican War. In 1848, he married Julia Dent and four years later was ordered to California with the 4th Infantry. Despondent over being separated from his wife and family, Grant started drinking and as a result was forced to resign from the service in 1854. From that time until the Civil War began, he would try farming in St. Louis, and working as a store clerk in Illinois, but for the man who had earned two brevet promotions for gallantry while fighting at Molino del Rey and Chapultepec during the Mexican War, neither job was satisfying and he failed miserably at both. In June of 1861, Grant was appointed a colonel by Governor Washburne of Illinois. Grant's experience in the Mexican War gave him a realistic view of what lay ahead, and his quiet tenacity and determination to win made him a dangerous opponent. His success in the western theater, most notably his brilliant triumph at Vicksburg, gained him national notice and the confidence of Abraham Lincoln who appointed him general in chief of all the Union armies. Grant's ability to coordinate Union forces fighting in the west while personally combating Lee in the east is a perfect example of his strategic versatility. After the war, Grant served as President of the United States for two terms. In 1884, eight years after leaving the White House, a banking venture left him penniless. Dying of throat cancer, and worried about the financial future of his family, Grant put his energy into writing his memoirs. A week after he finished his book, which was published by Mark Twain, the greatest general in the Union army passed away.

Griffin, Charles--A West Point graduate who served on the western frontier, Griffin was a veteran of the Mexican War and an instructor in artillery at West Point. During the Civil War, he commanded the Army of the Potomac's 1st Division, 5th Corps, later replacing General Warren as 5th Corps commander. A strict disciplinarian and aggressive fighter, he was quick to take the offense and often personally led his advancing troops into battle. Outspoken and possessing a caustic sense of humor, Griffin was respected by his peers and was popular with his men. After the war, he stayed on in the regular army and died of yellow fever in Galveston, in 1867.

   *Griffin held Joshua Chamberlain in high regard, as is evident in his letters of recommendation. Like General Warren, Griffin relied on Chamberlain a great deal during the last campaign of the war, and he was instrumental in Chamberlain's appointment by Grant for receiving the formal surrender at Appomattox. Upon his death, Griffin's cap, flag, bugle, and a sword that Chamberlain had given him when his own was lost during the last campaign, were sent to Joshua at Griffin's request. Chamberlain treasured the relics of his former commander and friend, and kept them on display in his library.

Hancock, Winfield Scott--From the onset of the war, this Union general established a reputation for being a skillful commander. Leading the 1st Division of the 2nd Corps of the Army of the Potomac, he distinguished himself at Antietam, Fredericksburg, and Chancellorsville. At Gettysburg, he played a vital role in securing the initial line of battle for the Union. On the second and third day at Gettysburg, he commanded the left center of the Union's line, helping to repulse Pickett's charge. It was during this action that he was severely wounded. After a lengthy recuperation, he resumed his command in March of the following year and contributed greatly in the battles of the Wilderness, Spottsylvania Court House, Cold Harbor, and Petersburg.

McClellan, George Brinton--Son of a well known surgeon and teacher, McClellan graduated second in his class at West Point and earned three brevets in the Mexican War for gallant and meritorious conduct. Resigning from the military in 1857, he became a successful railroad businessman. When the war began, he reentered the military as a Major General of Ohio volunteers. Shortly after the First Battle of Bull Run, he was placed in command of the Army of the Potomac, and did a remarkable job of organizing and training the army. Although McClellan's Penisular campaign was a failure, he was again put in charge of the armies in the eastern theater after General Pope was defeated at the Second Bull Run. His failure to pursue Lee after Antietam caused Lincoln to replace him with General Burnside. In 1864, McClellan ran against Lincoln for the presidencty and lost.

Meade, George Gordon--The son of a bussinessman and U.S. naval agent, Meade was born in Cadiz, Spain on December 31, 1815. Educated in Philadelphia and Washington, he graduated from West Point in 1835. Trained in artillary, he briefly served in the Second Seminole War. Resigning from the army to become a civil engineer, Meade was reinstated seven years later. In the Mexican War, he served as a topographic engineer, during which time he became aqainted with Robert E. Lee. During the Civil War, Meade proved to be a vital commander, his performance at Gettysburg being a perfect example. Unselfish and dedicated to the Union's cause, when General Grant came east, Meade offered to be replaced by Grant's right-hand man, General Sherman. Grant would later say, "This incident gave me even a more favorable opinion of Meade than did his great victory at Gettysburg the July before. It is men who wait to be selected, and not those who seek, from whom we may always expect the most efficient service."

Sheridan, Philip Henry--At West Point he was suspended for a year because of discipline problems, but graduated in 1853. He served with distinction in the Indian wars in Oregon. In 1863, he was made a major-general and commanded troops in the Chickamauga and Chattanooga campaigns. Recommended by Grant to command the Cavalry Corps of the Army of the Potomac, Sheridan led a brilliant campaign in the Shenadoah Valley and would later be instrumental in the last campaign of the war.

Sherman, William Tecumseh--A West Point graduate, and one of the Union's best generals, Sherman had a clear understanding of war, and what it took to win. Independent, unconventional, and brutally honest in his views, Sherman was Grant's right-hand man in the West as well as his trusted friend. Operating in the western theater, Sherman commanded troops in Kentucky and the army of Tennessee, with whom he distinguished himself at the Battle of Shiloh. He also played a vital role in the operations leading up to the surrender of Vicksburg. He is most remembered for his campaign on Atlanta and his famous "March to the Sea," which cut a fifty mile path of destruction through Georgia. His campaign from Savannah to Goldsboro, in which he marched his troops 425 miles in fifty days, is thought of by many to be his greatest achievement. When Grant was elected president in 1869, Sherman succeeded him as commander of the army, a position he held until 1883.

Warren, Gouverneur Kemble--Graduated second in a class of forty-four at West Point where he was promoted to the rank of Brevet Second Lieutenant in the Corps of Topographical

Engineers, July 1, 1850. Prior to the war, Warren served as an engineer on a number of surveys, including a hydrographical survey of the Mississippi Delta; he also taught Mathematics at West Point. Although mostly remembered for his actions at Gettysburg, where he played a pivotal role upon finding the Round Tops undefended, Warren's contributions as both an engineer and a commander were numerous. He was wounded both at the Battle at Gaines's Mill and at Gettysburg. He was promoted to Major General and put in command of the Second Corps from September of that year through March of 1864, at which time he took command of the Fifth Corps. During the last campaign, Warren was unjustly dismissed as 5th Corps commander by General Sheridan at Five Forks. Fourteen years after the war, Warren's case went to trial and he was exonerated of Sheridan's charges. After the war, he remained in the army for the rest of his life, working as an engineer.

*In Chamberlain's book The Passing Of the Armies, Joshua gives a detailed account of the events involving Warren, Sheridan, and Five Forks. During Warren's trial, Joshua testified on Warren's behalf.

Confederate President

Davis, Jefferson--Like Lincoln, Davis was born in a log cabin in Kentucky. He was the youngest of ten children, whose father named him after the President who was then in office--Thomas Jefferson. Davis spent his early childhood in Wilkinson County, just forty miles from the Mississippi River, where his father Samuel grew cotton and worked in the fields alongside his slaves. Davis graduated from Transylvania University, then West Point in 1828; twenty-third in a class of thirty-four. From the onset he showed promise as a soldier and served for seven years on the northwest frontier. He fought in the Black Hawk War and later distinguished himself during the Mexican War, in which he was herald a hero for his actions at Buena Vista. An excellent statesmen and debater, he began his political career in the House of Representatives and steadily worked his way up. Ambitious, organized, and always well informed, he served on the Senate from 1847 until 1851; as Secretary of War under President Franklin from 1853 to 1857; and again as a Senator from 1857 until January of 1861, when he resigned after his home state of Mississippi seceded from the Union. Davis, who had worked to preserve both slavery and the Union while in the Senate, was inaugurated President of the Confederate States on February 18, 1861, an office he would hold throughout the Civil War. Shortly after Lee's surrender at Appomattox, Davis was captured by Union troops near Irwinville, Georgia. For two years he was imprisoned at Fortress Monroe, charged with treason. In May of 1867, he was released on bail, and the charges against him were eventually dropped. His later years were spent writing Rise and Fall of the Confederate States, which was published in 1881, eight years before his death.

Confederate Generals

Hill, Ambrose Powell--A division under his command engaged with Buford's Union cavalry, touching off the battle of Gettysburg. Hill fought with distinction throughout the war and was killed at Petersburg, Virginia, on April 2, 1865.

Hood, John Bell--West Point graduate and commander of the legendary Texas Brigade, also called "Hood's Texans." Hood fought under both Jackson and Longstreet. At Gettysburg, he was wounded early in the action on the second day. Hood played an important role in the Battle of Chickamauga, where he lost his leg. During the remainder of the war, he would command troops in the western theater, replacing J. E. Johnston as the commander of the Army of Tennessee.

Jackson, Thomas J. (Stonewall)--West Point graduate, veteran of the Mexican War, and professor at Virginia Military Institute, this studious and deeply religious Confederate general's clear and precise understanding of warfare was a nightmare for the North. Implictitly trusted by Lee, the two generals made a formidable team. Hard driving and aggressive, Jackson's three month Shenandoah Valley Campaign is considered one of the most brilliant achievements in military history. Jackson earned his famous nickname at the first Battle of Manassas (Bull Run) when he and his brigade stood up against the Union forces like a "stone wall," an example that rallied Confederate troops to a powerful counterattack against the Yankees. After the battle of Chancellorsville, Jackson was accidentally shot by his own men and his left arm had to be amputated. Jackson's wish to die on a Sunday came true eight days later when he succumbed to pneumonia.

Johnston, Joseph E.--Graduated in the same West Point class as General Lee in 1829. A distinguished veteran of both the Mexican and Indian Wars, for which he earned four brevet promotions, Johnston would be wounded ten times in his military career. At different intervals during the Civil War, he commanded all the Confederate forces east of the Mississippi. Severely wounded at Seven Pines, Johnston was relieved by General Lee. Recovering from his injury, six months later, Johnston was given command of the Confederate forces in the western theater.

Lee, Robert E.--was born on January 19, 1807 in Westmoreland County, Virginia. Both his parents came from prominent families and his father was the famous 'Light Horse Harry' named so for his daring success as a cavalry commander during the American Revolution. Lee grew up in Alexandria, Virginia, and at the age of eighteen he entered West Point, graduating in 1829, second in his class. In June of 1831, he married Mary Randolph Custis, the great-granddaughter of Martha Washington. During the Mexican War, Lee served as a captain of engineers on the staff of General Winfield Scott, distinguishing himself as a competent and daring officer and earning three brevet promotions for his outstanding service at Cerro Gordo, Chapultepec, and Churubusco. From 1852 until 1855, Lee was superintendent at West Point, and in 1859, he commanded the troops that captured John Brown at Harper's Ferry. Although he did not believe in secession, at the outbreak of the war, Lee turned down Lincoln's offer to command the Union forces, unwilling to take up arms against his beloved state of Virginia. Resigning from the regular army, he joined the Confederate forces, and was commissioned as a major general of troops in Virginia. After General J.E. Johnston was wounded at Seven Pines, Lee took command of the Confederate armies in the eastern theater. He called his troops the Army of Northern Virginia, and brilliantly led them to many victories. Lee is regarded by most military critics to be the greatest general of the Civil War. His strategic genius, both on the offense and defense, was enhanced by his flexibility, daring, and ability to read his Union opponents. His greatest disadvantage was the North's greatest asset--numbers. Realizing this, Lee was forced to take greater risks than the enemy in order to defeat them; his victory at Chancellorsville is an excellent example. A man of integrity and honor, Lee was worshipped by his men and respected by his enemies, notably by the man who would eventually defeat him, Ulysses S. Grant. After the war, Lee became president of Washington College, later renamed Washington and Lee. Five years after the war ended, Lee, who said "The greatest mistake of my life was taking a military education," suffered a heart attack and died.

Longstreet, James--West Point graduate and veteran of the Mexican War, this Confederate general was referred to by Lee as his "Old War Horse," and by his troops as, "Old Pete." Hard fighting and steady on the battlefield, Longstreet's greatest talent rested in defensive warfare, an example being the Battle of Fredericksburg. Although he felt General Lee was partial to Virginians, Longstreet, who was born in South Carolina and raised in Georgia and Alabama, was always loyal to his commander, even when they disagreed at Gettysburg.

Pickett, George Edward--On the third day at Gettysburg, his division took the brunt of the slaughter. Early in the war, Pickett was severly wounded in the battle at Gaines's Mill. Near the end, of the war he commanded troops at Five Forks where he was defeated by Sheridan.

Stuart, James Ewell Brown (Jeb)--West Point graduate and outstanding Confederate cavalry commander, Stuart was the "eyes and ears" of Lee's army. Flamboyant and cocky, Stuart and his men had no competition for the first two years of the war and played havoc with the Union army. In the days leading up to Gettysburg, Stuart, who was trying to ride around Hooker's army, ended up loosing contact with General Lee for ten days, and it proved costly (he didn't arrive until the evening of the second day of battle). Stuart was wounded while trying to stop Sheridan's cavalry at Yellow Tavern (near Richmond) on May 11, 1864, and died a day later.

Glossary

Artillery--cannons and other large-caliber weapons. The term is also used in reference to the troops that handle those weapons. During the Civil War, the Napoleon 12-pounder was the most common cannon used. This bronze-barreled smooth-bore weapon fired off twelve-pound shots and were an effective destructive force, especially against infantry at short range. It usually took a team of six horses to pull the cannon onto the battlefield and a crew of five soldiers to man them.

Battery--usually consisted of six cannons and crews. The term was also used to refer to the fortified position where the cannons were placed.

Bayonet--(socket) had three fluted sides and a needle-sharp point for spearing. Bayonets were attached to the rifle with relative ease but were not routinely used in combat. In camp, the bayonet was used to hold candles or as a cooking tool.

Black Hat Brigade--see Iron Brigade.

Brevet Rank--a commission promoting an officer in rank without an increase in pay or authority; regarded as an honorary title awarded for gallant or meritorious action in time of war.

Butterfield's Light Brigade--3rd Brigade, 1st Division, Fifth Corps of the Army of the Potomac. Named after its commander General Daniel Butterfield, who composed the bugle "lights out" call, known as 'Taps'. Butterfield's Light Brigade was known for its camaraderie and had earned a reputation as being good fighters. When the 20th Maine joined its ranks in September of 1862, Butterfield was no longer its commander.

Cavalry--these troops were trained to fight on horseback. They were primarily used for both scouting and screening an army's movements. In the first two years of the war, the Confederate cavalry, led by men like Jeb Stuart and Nathan Bedford Forrest, was far superior to that of the North, but with time, the Union cavalry under the command of generals like Sheridan and Buford equalized the opposing forces.

Emancipation Proclamation--was enacted on January 1, 1863 and "proclaimed that all slaves in areas still in a state of rebellion were hence forward, free." With his proclamation, President Lincoln shifted the focus of the war. The war had begun its fight over state and union rights; now, with the Emancipation Proclamation, it defined a new and moral cause to justify the destruction and bloodshed--the abolishment of human slavery. With the enactment of this proclamation, the Confederacy's chances of insuring support from European countries like

England were greatly weakened. Two years later, on February 1, 1865 President Lincoln signed the 13th Amendment which gave the Emancipation Proclamation "constitutional backbone."

Flank--the right or left side of a military formation. For example, on the second day of battle at Gettysburg, Lee's plan was to attack both of Meade's flanks--the right and left sides of Meade's line along Cemetery Ridge.

Greenback Party--A political party in America that was active between 1876 and 1884. The party took its name from "greenbacks" which were paper notes used as currency during and following the Civil War.

Hardtack--made of flour, salt, and water, these flat biscuit squares measured about three inches in diameter and were about a half an inch thick. A ration of hardtack, which was considered nutritious, usually consisted of nine or ten biscuits. These were so hard that the only way a soldier could eat them was to break them up with his rifle butt, or soften them up in his coffee. Although hardtack often became moldy and wormy, it still remained the mainstay of a soldiers diet.

Homeopathic Physician--A Doctor who practices homeopathic medicine. Homeopathy was introduced in 1796 by a German physician named Samuel Hahnemann and was a popular alternative to standard medical treatments during the 1800's. Homeopathic physicians believe that "like cures like", in other words, a substance that produces certain symptoms in a healthy person will cure those symptoms in a sick patient. For example, onions induce crying and a runny nose, thus a homeopathic physician would use onions to treat patient with a cold.

Infantry--foot soldiers.

Iron Brigade--One of the most famous brigades in the Civil War, it was originally made up of 2nd, 6th, and 7th Wisconsin and the 19th Indiana regiments under the command of General John Gibbon. It got its nick-name "Black Hat Brigade" because the men wore non-regulation black hats. Under Gibbon, this brigade first distinguished itself at the 2nd Battle of Bull Run while fighting against Stonewall Jackson's troops. Their reputation as hard fighters grew with each battle they fought. The 24th Michigan joined its ranks right before the Antietam campaign, and it was at Antietam that a reporter dubbed them the Iron Brigade. Great credit is given to the Iron Brigade for its gallant effort on Seminary Ridge during the first day of battle at Gettysburg. At Gettysburg the Iron Brigade lost over two thirds of its men, and would never recover its former effectiveness.

Minie Ball--A lead bullet designed by French Army Captain Minie in 1849. Used for muzzle-loading rifles, the Minie ball allowed a soldier to shoot with accuracy a distance of 250 yards. This bullet, which was only an inch in length, would spin through the grooved rifle barrels, and that spinning motion allowed it to travel farther and with more accuracy. Weighing only two ounces, these bullets expanded upon impact and caused extensive damage; bones shattered by Minie balls (arms and legs) had to be amputated; gut shots were almost always fatal.

Paris Exposition of 1878--International World fair which took place in Paris, France. Covering an area of sixty-four acres, exhibits of fine art, machinery, and domestic architecture were represented by nations from all over the world.

Picket--a detachment of one or more soldiers whose duty was to guard the front lines and warn commanders of enemy movement and/or advance.

Pontoon--a flat-bottomed boat, usually made of wood and used to either ferry troops across water or as supports for temporary bridges.

Reconnaissance--mission of locating the enemy, surveying their territory, estimating their number, and determining their intentions.

Sharpshooter--expert marksmen, these soldiers usually acted as snipers. Using height and cover to their advantage, they would hide in trees or nestle themselves among rocks. The Sharpshooters Rifle (a target rifle) was sometimes equipped with telescopic sights which magnified small objects at a distance, allowing them to zero in on officers and artillerymen.

Theaters of War--During the Civil War, the country was geographically divided into two areas of military operation--the eastern and western theaters. The eastern theater included the terrain extending from the Appalachian Mountains east to the Atlantic Ocean. The western theater included the terrain extending from the Appalachian Mountains west to the Mississippi River.

Underground Railroad--A network of escape routes used by run away slaves as they traveled to the free states in the North and to Canada. Supported by Abolitionists and religious groups, such as the Quakers, this loosely organized system used railroad terms for code words--safe houses where slaves could hide were called "stations"; "conductors" were the people who transported the slaves from one station to the next.

Bibliography

Books   (listed by author; collective works by title)

African Americans VOICES of TRIUMPH. Time-Life Books, Alexandria, Virginia, 1993.

Benedick, Michael Les, The Impeachment and Trial of Andrew Johnson. Norton, New York, 1973.

Boatner, Mark M., The Civil War Dictionary. David McKay Company, Inc., New York, 1959.

Catton, Bruce, The American Heritage Picture History of THE CIVIL WAR. American Heritage/Wing Books, New York, Avenel, New Jersey, 1988.

Chamberlain, Joshua L., "Bayonet! Forward" My Civil War Reminiscences. Stan Clark Military Books, Gettysburg, Pennsylvania, 1994.

Chamberlain, Joshua L., The Passing of the Armies. Stan Clark Military Books, Gettysburg, Pennsylvania, 1994. First published by G.H. Putnam, New York, 1915.

Chamberlain, Joshua L., Through Blood & Fire at Gettysburg. Stan Clark Military Books, Gettysburg, Pennsylvania, 1994. First published by Cosmopolitan Magazine, New York, 1912.

Cleaveland, Nehemiah, History of Bowdoin Colledge with Biographical Sketches of its Graduates. James Ripley Osgood & Company, Boston, 1882.

Clifford, Harold B., Maine and Her People. The Bond Wheelwright Company, Freeport, Maine, 1976.

Desjardin, Thomas A., Stand Firm Ye Boys From Maine. Thomas Publications, Gettysburg PA, 1995.

Foote, Shelby, The Civil War A Narrative Vol. 2 Fredericksburg to Meridian; Stars in Their Courses. Random House, New York, 1963.

Golay, Michael, To Gettysburg and Beyond. Crown Publishers, INC., New York, 1994.

Greenleaf, Moses, A Survey of the State of Maine In Reference to its Geographical features, Statistics and Political Economy. Shirley and Hyde, Portland, Me., 1829.

Hatch, Louis C., The History of Bowdoin College. Loring, Short& Harman, Portland, Maine, 1927.

Johnson, Swafford, Great Battles of THE CIVIL WAR Northern Victories. Crescent Books, New York, 1991.

Lawson, William, Maine to the Wilderness, The Civil War Letters of Pvt. William Lawson, 20th Maine Infantry. Publisher's Press, Orange Virginia, 1993.

Long, Richard A., Black AMERICANA. Chartwell Books, Inc., New Jersey, 1985.

Lord, Francis, A., Civil War Collector's Encyclopedia. Castle Books, New York, 1965.

Maine At Gettysburg, Report of Maine Commissioners; Prepared by The Executive Committee. The Lakeside Press Engravers, Printers and Binders, Portland, Maine, 1898.

Minot, John Clair and Snow, Donald Francis, Tales of Bowdoin. Press of Kennebec Journal, Augusta, Maine, 1901.

Mitchell, Lt. Col. Joseph B., Military Leaders in the Civil War. G.P. Putman's Sons, New York, 1972.

Munson, Gorham, Penobscot Down East Paridise. J.B. Lippincott Company, Philadelphia, New York, 1959.

Nesbitt, Mark, Ghosts of Gettysburg. Thomas Publications, Gettysburg, Pennsylvania, 1991.

North, James W., The History Of Augusta Maine. New England History Press, Somersworth, 1981.

Norton, Oliver Willcox, The Attack and Defense of Little Round Top. Stan Clark Military Books, Gettysburg, Pennsylvania, 1992.

Oberholtzer, Ellis Paxson, History of the United States SINCE THE CIVIL WAR Vol 2. Macmillan Company, New York, 1928.

Pullen, John J., The Twentieth Maine A Volunteer Regiment In The Civil War. Morningside House, Inc., Dayton, Ohio, 1991.

Religion at Bowdoin College: A History. Bowdoin, College, Bunswick, Maine, 1981.

Rhodes, Robert Hunt, All For The Union. (Forward; Ward, Georffrey C.) Orion Books, New York, 1985.

Stowe, Harriet Beecher, Uncle Tom's Cabin. The library of America, New York, 1982.

Styple, William B., With a Flash of His Sword. Belle Grove Pub., Kearny, New Jersey, 1994.

THE WAY TO APPOMATTOX Battles and Leaders of the Civil War. Castle Books, New York, 1956.

The Volume Library 2. The Southwestern Company, Nashville, Tennessee, 1988.

The Wabanakis of Maine and the Maritimes. Maine Indian Program, Bath, Maine, 1989.

Tucker, Glenn, Lee and Longstreet at Gettysburg. Bobbs-Merrill Company, Indianapolis, Kanas City, New York, 1968.

Trial of Andrew Johnson. Vol 1. Government Printing Office, Washington, D.C., 1868.

Trulock, Alice Rains, In the Hands of Providence Joshua L. Chamberlain & the American Civil War. The University of North Carolina Press, North Carolina, 1992.

Wallace, Willard M., Soul Of The Lion A Biography Of General Joshua L. Chamberlain. Stan Clark Military Books, Gettysburg, Pennsylvania, 1991.

Ward, Geoffrey C. (with Ric and Ken Burns), THE CIVIL WAR An Illustrated History. Knopf, New York, 1990.

Wilson, Charles Morrow, Aroostook: Our Last Frontier. Stephen Daye Press, Brattleboro, Vermont, 1937.

Windrow, Martin, The Civil War Rifleman. Franklin Watts, New York, London, Toronto, Sydney, 1985.

Newspapers

Bangor Daily News, Thurs., June 29, 1989: Brewer's Joshua Chamberlain; Brian Swartz.

Eastern Argus, Friday, Jan. 3, 1868: Governor's Address.

The Times Record, Brunswick, Maine, Thurs., Aug. 3, 1978: Bowdoin's scholar-soldier An Innovative college president; Richard L. Sherman.

Evening Post, Sept, 1869, article on Chamberlain's reelection. (Chamberlain files, Pejepscot Historical Society, Brunswick, Maine)

Lewiston Journal, Oct., 3, 1942:Chamberlains, Maine History Fame, Were Opposed in Polititcs; Sam E. Conner.

New-York Tribune, June 29-July 7, 1863: The Rebel Invasion; General Meade Occupies Hanover and York; The Great Battle Imminent; Strenghth Of Lee's Army; Severe Battle Near Geyysburg; Heavy Attack on our First Army Corps; The First Day's Fighting; Desperate Rush of the Enemy for the Best Position; The Fighting At Gettysburg; The Severest Actions of the War; Longstreet Taken Prisoner; Advantage on Our Side; General Sickles Loses A Leg; The Great Victory; The Rebel Army Totally Defeated; Twenty Thousand Prisoners Captured; The Rebels Pause-Waver-Break and Scatter; A great and Glorious Victory for the Potomac Army.

The New York Times, Saturday, July 4, 1863: Official Dispatches From Gen. Mead; The Battle of Wednesday; The Battle of Thursday; Yesterday's Battle.
The Portland Transcript, April, 1968, (Johnson's impeachment trial) Events Of The Week.

The Portland Transcript, May 9, 1868: Matters in Maine.

Portland Press Herald, August, 20, 1961: Twelve Days That Shook Maine; Fred Humiston.

The Sunday Times, (Portland) January, 18, 1880, No.25:

Articles from the Chamberlain files Pejepscot Historical Society, Brunswick, Maine: Joshua Chamberlain A known name in Brewer (Howard Kenney); Whipped For Chewing Tobacco; The Chamberlain Bracelet; Gov. Chamberlain our next U.S. Senator; Mighty Mite Of Faculty Beat Bowdoin '62 Grads To Colors (Franklin P. Lincoln);Chamberlain--A Sketch.
Governor Chamberlain Addresses: 1867, 1868, 1869, 1870: (Augusta; Stevens & Sayward, printers to the State: Augusta: Sprague, Owen & Nash, printers to the State)

Magazines and Pamphlets

Bowdoin Vol. 64, No.1 Spring/Summer Issue: Rediscovering Joshua Chamberlain; "Do it! That's How".

Gettysburg, information booklet published by Tem Inc.

Gettysburg Times, Sep. 1994.

Gettysburg: Gettysburg Travel Council brochure.

Gettysburg: Official Map and Guide; National Park Service.

Joshua L. Chamberlain's Brunswick: Pejepscot Historical Society.

Joshua Lawrence Chamberlain Museum: Pejepscot Historical Society.

Joshua Lawrence Chamberlain 1828-1914 A Sesquicentennial Tribute; Richard L. Sherman; Brunswick Publishing Company, 1978.

Tour Book, New Jersey/Pennsylvania: AAA, American Automobile Association.

Towerguide: National Tower guide/ Gettysburg National Park.

Big Round Top: Gettysburg National Military Park pamphlet.

Map & Guide for Brewer: Chamber of Commerce.

Acknowledgments

In the course of writing this book I have the had the help and support of many people. I would like to thank--my nephew, John Hamlin Deans for requesting that I write the book; my husband John, for his patience and encouragement; my daughters, Jessica, Rachel, and Emma, for the sacrifices they had to make due to my writing, and for their unconditional love; and to my mother, who has always believing in me.

The writing of this book has been made easier by the efforts of those biographers whose works have paved the way before me. My indebtedness and admiration must be noted to authors--Alice Rains Trulock, In the Hands of Providence, Joshua L. Chamberlain And The American Civil War; Willard M. Wallace, Soul Of The Lion, A Biography Of General Joshua L. Chamberlain; and John J. Pullen, The Twentieth Maine, A Volunteer Regiment In The Civil War.

A special note of thanks to the staff at the Pejepscot Historical Society in Brunswick, Maine. Especially to its curator, Julia Colvin Oehmig, for her valuable time, expertise, and continual encouragement. To Pelle Rosenquist and Jim Cabot, who always made me feel welcome at the Chamberlain Museum. To Dianne M. Gutscher, curator of Special Collections at Bowdoin's Hawthorne-Longfellow Library, and to her assistant Susan Ravdin. To Librarian Thomas Bennett, who works in the Portland Room at the Portland Public Library, and who helped me on numerous occasions; to the staff at Baxter Library in Gorham, Maine, especially Linda Straw and Pam Turner. To Holly Hurd-Forsyth at the Maine Historical Society in Portland, and to Earl Shuttleworth of the Maine Historic Preservation Committee. To my guide at Gettysburg National Park, Anthony Nicastro, for making me realize the "bigger picture."

For their valuable input upon reading the manuscript, and for their corrections, suggestions, and encouragement, sincere gratitude goes to: writer-editors, John Cofran and Wanda Poor Whitten; Chamberlain expert, Julia Covin Oehmig; editor and author, William B. Styple; Dr. Anne Leonard, retired Professor of History, Memphis State University; for their historical expertise, Jim Nevins and Bob Crickenberger. For graciously allowing me to use photographs from their personal collections, a special thanks to James Frasca and Bedford Hayes.

Thank you again to all the before mentioned, and to those others who have offered their support and help along the way.